Enjoy the Fu@king Journey

Stories, Ideas, and Concepts written to remind you to simply enjoy your time on this earth.

To:

My Team at The Thompson Group
Past, Present, and Future.

Thank you for joining me on my
journey.

Foreword

Welcome to my eighth book! Most folks are impressed to find I'm a published author, but the publishing world has transformed like many things these last few years. Having a book published is not that big of a deal. If you like this one, you can find my first other books on Amazon.com.

I hope you find my stories and ideas helpful. Most are written early morning and have some tie to a recent event or thought. I've always written for myself, but with the amount of content that comes from my mind, I finally thought, "why not share?"

After a 2 plus years of sobriety, I decided to pick back up the bottle. Some of these words were written with the ache of a morning head while others were written with clarity.

The sober life was amazing and will one day return, but for now, I'm enjoying my old friend and keeping her in check.

When I'm unable to continue with my friendly relationship and my friendship turns to a relationshit, I shall recuse myself yet again.   But for now, cheers.

I write between 500 and 1000 words 300 plus days a year. This book includes my thoughts and ideas from 2017. I have enough content for 5 more books and I add to that every morning. If you like my work, tell your friends and family; if you don't like my work, keep your comments to yourself. No need to push your negative thoughts on others.

Thanks for allowing me to share a little of me with you and I encourage your comments. If you could send me a note at ninja@thethompsongroup.net I would be honored to hear your thoughts.

Anson R. Thompson
10/17

Chapter List

Attention Lazy People – Contribute!

"If you assume that there is no hope, you guarantee that there will be no hope. If you assume that there is an instinct for freedom, that there are opportunities to change things, then there is a possibility that you can contribute to making a better world."
— **Noam Chomsky**

Do you contribute? Seriously, do you contribute? Do you add to the art of our world? Do you employ others? Do you provide positive content and ideas to your society?

So much of our society does not contribute. They suck, drain, and pull from those of us that work.

Do you work? Do you add to the labor force; do you add your hands and mind to today's ideas and help move society forward?

Do you live? Do you contribute to your community?   Do you volunteer to your little league, church, or local nonprofit?

Do you care for others?

Do you give to others?

Do you contribute?

There are people in this country that can walk, talk, and hold a job, yet they refuse to work, instead opting for government subsidies, hand-outs, and free cheese.

My sister has one leg; she's going to retire at 57 years old. She and her husband, Dr. Ken, worked their asses off to build wealth and position themselves to do what they want at 57 years old.

Will Dr. Ken continue to practice, probably, but they will have the choice to live comfortably off their savings and earnings until they die at a ripe old age.

Did I mention my sister has one leg?

If you have two legs, you have an advantage over my sister, but yet, she's kicking ass and taking names.

Do you contribute?

What do you do every day? What do you spend your time doing? My sister spends her time doing accounting work, helping run her husband's dental practice and also is an accomplished editor of a few books on Amazon.

According to the U.S. Department of Labor:

Year	Jan	Feb	Mar	Apr	May	Jun	Jul	Aug	Sep	Oct	Nov	Dec
2007	4.6	4.5	4.4	4.5	4.4	4.6	4.7	4.6	4.7	4.7	4.7	5.0
2008	5.0	4.9	5.1	5.0	5.4	5.6	5.8	6.1	6.1	6.5	6.8	7.3
2009	7.8	8.3	8.7	9.0	9.4	9.5	9.5	9.6	9.8	10.0	9.9	9.9
2010	9.8	9.8	9.9	9.9	9.6	9.4	9.4	9.5	9.5	9.4	9.8	9.3
2011	9.1	9.0	9.0	9.1	9.0	9.1	9.0	9.0	9.0	8.8	8.6	8.5
2012	8.3	8.3	8.2	8.2	8.2	8.2	8.2	8.1	7.8	7.8	7.7	7.9
2013	8.0	7.7	7.5	7.6	7.5	7.5	7.3	7.3	7.2	7.2	6.9	6.7
2014	6.6	6.7	6.7	6.2	6.3	6.1	6.2	6.2	5.9	5.7	5.8	5.6
2015	5.7	5.5	5.4	5.4	5.5	5.3	5.2	5.1	5.0	5.0	5.0	5.0
2016	4.9	4.9	5.0	5.0	4.7	4.9	4.9	4.9	4.9	4.8	4.6	4.7
2017	4.8	4.7	4.5	4.4	4.3							

The current unemployment rate is 4.3%. Businesses are clamoring for workers. Why is 4.3% of the people refusing or unable to work?

I don't know. I don't have any idea why someone would live life sans of value. Work gives life value. For God's sake, work or contribute.

I spent my day working on validation reports for my team. I'm trying to get all my sale's folk to a point of self-sustaining. Once they hit their mark, they can earn unlimited amounts of money.

I did some planning. I did some hard work. I spent my day with my Queen planning for the last few days of this week. We reviewed sales, projections, and worked on our company.

We contributed, we planned to add employees, we planned to send some of our team out to our Colorado operations. We bantered back and forth about our next moves and how we might make a major move in one of our markets that could radically change our position.

Please, contribute. If you contribute, society wins. If society wins, I win, if others win, you win. The more we win, the more we win.

Contribution is the key to success of our society. Stop bitching, moaning, and whining about your plight, station, or space in our society. It is up to each individual to reshape society. It is not up to government, nor business, it is incumbent on us, we the people, to contribute our specific skill sets to build a better world.

Just contribute.

"If you assume that there is no hope, you guarantee that there will be no hope. If you assume that there is an instinct for freedom, that there are opportunities to change things, then there is a possibility that you can contribute to making a better world."
— **Noam Chomsky**

For the ones that can't seem to get there on time...

"It is never too late to be what you might have been."
— **George Eliot**

Hello, I'm talking to you from a position of success. I pride myself on being on time and think it might be the time you thought about this little issue.

I wanted to talk to you about your continual lateness.

It's embarrassing, it's not professional, and sets the tone for everything else you do.

Shit happens, but it doesn't happen every time you are supposed to be somewhere at a specific time.

Since you can't seem to get your shit together, let's just set 5 rules moving forward:

1. If you are going to be late, call or text; no exceptions.
2. Plan on arriving 15 minutes before your appointment time. Arriving 15 minutes gives you time to review notes, mentally prepare for whatever type meeting you

are attending; it's key to looking professional.

3. Look at your calendar every evening for the next day. If you are old, look at your paper. If you are young, look at your phone. Make sure you know where you are going and what time you are to be there.

4. Get up earlier, if you are always late, you are starting your morning behind the 8 ball. I got up at 4 am today, 2 am yesterday and 5 am most days. I've had 3 of the most productive days I've experienced in a long time. If you're not a morning person, sorry, find another author.

5. Set Alarms. Your phone has an alarm, if you are up a little earlier, in the morning set a 30-minute reminder before every appointment. I do this when flying so I don't drink too much tequila and miss boarding.

Follow those rules. You might disagree, but I speak from a position of success.

If you are involved in a group, you always have that one or two people that can't seem to make the meeting on time, every damn time.

Use this as a discussion starter next meeting, get input from your group. If you are to start at 8:00, everyone needs to be seated at 8:00.

You know that couple that shows up late to church, every week, that's who I'm talking

about. You make it on time every week, why
can't they?

It's very disrespectful to the rest of the group to
be late every damn time.

Again, shit happens, and that is the exception
to reality. If you leave and plan on arriving 15
minutes early, you can accommodate most
closed roads, trains, or accidents.

Stop being late, it's unbecoming and makes you
look like a slug of a human. I don't like doing
business with people that are always late and
I'm not alone.

Show up late at your own peril. You've been
warned, it's important, and if this offends you I
might ask, "Why does this offend you?"

"It is never too late to be what you might have
been."
— **George Eliot**

Bad News – People Don't Like YOU... and it's OK!

"You must remember, family is often born of blood, but it doesn't depend on blood. Nor is it exclusive of friendship. Family members can be your best friends, you know. And best friends, whether or not they are related to you, can be your family."
— **Trenton Lee Stewart**

Well, I've got some bad news for you. There are a lot of folks that simply don't like you.

There are some people that don't like you if:

You're Fit
You're Fat
You're Lazy
You Work Hard
You're White
You're Black
You're Male
You're Gay
You're Straight
You're Bi...

I could go on, but here's the thing. No matter who you are, you start from a position of dislike from some people. No matter who you are, where you are from, or what you look like.

I'm a writer, I write stuff. I think that my words resonate with about 1% of my readers daily. That's 99% that read my work most days and think "this sucks."

But yet I continue to write. Every day, I get up, I pen a few thoughts. It's a gift, I know. To mind stream words that might or might not touch one person.

But I know that occasionally, my words reach those for whom they are intended. I have proof. Impacting one person a day is worth the time I spend dumping my mind. Truth be told, I don't do this for anyone but me which at times is painfully obvious to my readers.

I write for my 1% and I'm asking you to consider connecting with your 1%. Can we all begin living for those that we were intended?

Most people live their life trying to please everyone, but that's impossible. My uncle Jake used to say "you can't be Jesus Christ to everyone." He's right. A great lesson for a young person or maybe an old person.

That quote just lost me some readers. If you're still with me, thank you. If you are gone, good riddance.

My personal coach told me, "I think you offend people at times." I said, "in what way?"

He said, "you have no tolerance for anyone that does not believe they are in total control of their own success. You seem to lack sympathy."

I replied, "f-word them." My Dad asked that I quit using the F word. That's for you pop.

But my coach is coaching me to be better and maybe he can teach me how to be more sympathetic. There's always hope.

But I digress.

A lot of people love you, but there are a shit ton that do not! And that is ok. Actually, it's great. Imagine everyone you saw wanted to talk to you, touch you, and steal your time.

Your time is valuable and not everyone has earned your time. Don't fret the folks that don't connect with you. Thank them, your life is far less complex having a few detractors.

Be nice. Always be nice. But don't think you have to be liked by everyone. I'm a white straight male. That alone makes me hated all over the world just by that description.

You have a small audience. Figure out your audience and target them. These are your people. Your best friends are the people you have yet to meet.

Don't settle for half-ass friendships, go find your tribe. They are out there waiting for you to find them. Quit being a sissy, get up, get out, and find your people!

Last year, I made some new friends. A bunch actually. I love these people. My new friend Paul, is my buddy. My new friend, Josh, and his cool wife, Paula. Casey, Jeremy, Devyn, Danny, and I reconnected with Rudi. I met some amazing new folks last year.

I now have many friends in Colorado. I've met some of the most awesome people I've ever met in my 47 years on this earth in Colorado. Steve P, Dan M, Bobby D. and even Jimmy G. I've met an amazing woman in Linda M, a couple of Chris's, B and C and a man named Ed that has a weird last name.

I could go on. But my point is, seek and ye shall find. There are people in your life you are tolerating. Stop tolerating. You are what you tolerate.

You don't need to buy a home five states away to find your tribe, you are surrounded by amazing people YOU do not know in your community.

Stop trying to be Jesus Christ to everyone. Pick your people, pick your tribe and expand your horizons.

My life is fuller because I don't try and please the masses. I'm not for everyone and truth be told, neither are you.

So, be nice, but be free. Know that not every human likes you and acknowledges its okay not to like every other person you know.

There are some big frigging duds out there. Let me tell you. I've worked with a few.

Well, it's evening. I'm on a train from the airport to my condo in Denver. I'm not sure how many people live in our building, but I'm sure there are some of my people there.

I'll be nice. I'll smile and start a conversation and maybe this week I can add a friend, or two, or fifty.

Never forget you are valuable, but the value has a different meaning to different people. To some, you are valuable to a fine work of art and to others your value is akin to a losing lottery ticket.

Free yourself of the idea that everyone does, did, or should like you and start living a life of freedom and friends.

You are not for everyone and that's OK...

"You must remember, family is often born of blood, but it doesn't depend on blood. Nor is it exclusive of friendship. Family members can be your best friends, you know. And best friends, whether or not they are related to you, can be your family."
— **Trenton Lee Stewart**

3 Things, 5:15 AM Call and Getting Sober

"A learning experience is one of those things that says, 'You know that thing you just did? Don't do that."
— **Douglas Adams**

We all have three things.

Three things we need to improve, change, or eliminate from our lives.

My partner and I did some mid-year planning. We typically sit down in January and in June and review financials, speak openly and honestly about operations and what changes we need to make.

Yesterday, we reviewed our plans with our coach and he drilled down our plan into 3 specific action items.

We now have a roadmap to follow to take very specific actions to improve our company.

As I was writing these words, my phone just rang. It's 5:15 am in the morning. Who calls at 5:15 am?

It was a client, she had just gotten her insurance bill and asked if we could check her rate. She's had a couple of losses, but thinks her rates is out of line and wanted "someone to check it out."

I sent an email to my personal lines team and they will get to work making sure that we have her best rate and coverage.

Our mission statement is find the pain, heal the pain, show the love. It's time to show a little love.

But I digress.

What are 3 things you need to improve in your company or in your life? Think; we all have areas we need to improve.

Maybe it's your health, maybe it's your relationship with your significant other, or maybe it's your consumption of booze.

I've fought the battle with booze most of my life. Taking years off, getting sober and then diving right back into my love and admiration of the spirits.

I'm enjoying my ride with alcohol at the moment, but will soon take a hiatus.

Because of my history, I get contacted every so often from a friend that wants to quit drinking. I have successfully stopped for extended periods of time so I can help others that want to "get off the sauce."

A few days ago, I got a text message from a good friend that had decided to take a hiatus from fermented beverages.

I get these calls occasionally. As good as I am at drinking, I'm also a "sober professional." Her message yesterday was: "Today has been the hardest day so far. My entire body aches. Irritable, happy my mind is clear and I have a positive attitude about days to come."

I responded with "go for a walk, maybe a run. Move, eat quality foods, stop eating trash. Google "living sober" there are a lot of folks that can help you on your path.

"Ann" is making changes in her life to improve her relationships with others. It's a noble fight, one that should be commended, but that's Ann's area of improvement.

Ann is not alone and having lived for 48 years, I know that life ebbs and flows.

Ask yourself what are 3 things you can improve upon in your life or business. Formulate a game plan and get some action steps that can help you achieve your goals.

You are not alone, we all have areas we need to improve.

It's Tuesday morning, it's an amazing day, and it's time to get to work!

Pick your 3 things, answer the phone whenever it rings, and if you need to quit drinking, quit drinking. I did, I have, and for me, that has made all the difference.

"A learning experience is one of those things that says, 'You know that thing you just did? Don't do that."
— **Douglas Adams**

How to Squeeze 5 days into 4. A Celebration of Accomplishment

"It had long since come to my attention that people of accomplishment rarely sat back and let things happen to them. They went out and happened to things."
— **Leonardo da Vinci**

5:03 am, coconut oil infused coffee in hand and I'm ready to start this short week.

It's Tuesday although many of us will mistake it for a Monday. It tastes and smells like a Monday, but that was yesterday.

Yesterday we hiked, ate, drank, cooked, ate, and drank a little more. It was a holiday weekend, we squeezed every drop of juice out of these last few days.

But time to get to work, time to buckle down, time to build and kill "my list."

There have been times in my life where I needed to buckle up, dive back in, reengage. This is not one of those times, but when I tend to get serious about life, work, and play I have my trusty list.

So, dear reader, it's a short week; what will you accomplish? If you want to have an impact, use a little list.

Grab a napkin, old worn piece of paper, or maybe even a paper plate. Write down the things you need to do, and get busy. Take 20 minutes out of your day, your morning, whilst you drink your coffee, and simply write down "things I will do in this short week."

And then simply list all the stuff you need to do. What clients need to be contacted, what staff member needs some attention, where should you direct your energy for the most impact?

Some people are reading this and thinking "of course I will have my list," but others are thinking "lists are silly.".

No matter where you fall on the "list" spectrum, give it a shot.

I could go on, but I've got to get working on my list. I've got another day out West and then will be returning home to meet with our Midwest clients, staff, and friends.

Good luck, you only have 4 days to do 5 days of work, so get busy. As you mark things off, you'll get a little sense of accomplishment. Each item completed is a little celebration.

Join me in a celebration of accomplishment.

"It had long since come to my attention that people of accomplishment rarely sat back and let things happen to them. They went out and happened to things."
— **Leonardo da Vinci**

517% Happier – Changing the World just a little bit.

"Never doubt that a small group of thoughtful, committed, citizens can change the world. Indeed, it is the only thing that ever has."
— **Margaret Mead**

4:42 am, coconut infused coffee in hand and I'm ready to change the world.

If you think about it, it does not take much to change the world. A smile to a stranger, a compliment to your co-worker, or maybe some fresh flowers for your partner or spouse from your local grocery store.

You, yes you, can change the world today. Start small. Engage your waitress this morning and tell her she looks nice.

If you choose to eat breakfast at home, leave a note for your wife or partner reminding them how much you love them.

Call your kids today. All of them, reach out and remind them how damn proud of them you are.

Write and email or send a handwritten note to an old friend to brighten up their day.

I think in this time of upheaval, the little things, the important things get overlooked.

Instead of making that post which effectively angers half the people in your life, share some positive news about your life. Yes, you do have positive news going on in your life.

Imagine if everyone today, just took today and was 17% happier. Not 20%, not 10%, but 17% happier.

It does not take much to be 17% happier. Most people live their life angry, upset, and confused so why not shine a light on your fellow man or woman and let them see just a little hope.

Shoot rays of hope from your eyes, your smile, and your actions. Help others see the good today. There are a hundred ways you can bring joy to the world, but you have to try.

How can you change the world? Just today. Not in a big way, not in a way that would start a movement or have people wearing funny hats, but what can you do to bring a little positive to the world?

Donate to charity. Buy a stranger's lunch, hand a few dollars to someone in need, but do something, anything to add to the positive of this world.

This is not a movement; this is a request. I'm asking you, my friend, my reader, the consumer of my words to do just a little something today that will brighten another human's day.

Pick up that special drink from Starbucks for your assistant on the way to work. Buy doughnuts for your office. Tell your manager how much you appreciate their leadership.

Don't lie, there are too many great opportunities to be totally truthful and make someone feel just a little better about their life.

It's hump day. It's the middle of the week, and just two days from Friday, think about that. The weekend is coming, just 48 hours and the joy of a couple free days will arrive just in time for you to recharge your batteries.

Do a great job today. Leave your job thinking, "that was the best work I've done in years."

Focus, commit to making today 17% better than every other day this week, maybe this month, maybe even this year.

Fuel up with good food. Don't eat crap today. Avoiding crap processed sugar-filled food will make you 17% happier. Give it a shot.

Maybe pass on that after work cocktail or joint or pill or whatever you use to "change your state." Enjoy your clarity of mind.

Start a book, download a new podcast, or find a quote that you can share with a couple people to brighten their day.

Come on people, changing the world is not that hard. It sounds overwhelming, but I'm here to tell you it's the little things that can brighten up our world.

I'm off to talk pretty. I need to share some knowledge with some people that need to know what I know.

I might make them laugh a little, I might bring a little humor to a topic that is pretty dry, but I'm going to moisten the topic up, just a little.

We all have opportunities to make our world a little better place.

I'm asking you, well, begging you to bring your A game today. Be a little better, do a little better job, smile a little more and help me make our world just a little better place for all human beings.

You may say I'm a dreamer, but I'm not the only one. I hope one day you will join me by making our world 17% happier.

"Never doubt that a small group of thoughtful, committed, citizens can change the world. Indeed, it is the only thing that ever has."
— **Margaret Mead**

That Dreaded 2:11 am Call

"If you love someone but rarely make yourself available to him or her that is not true love."
— **Thich Nhat Hanh**

The only thing that separates you from your competition is your availability. If you can be available for your clients no matter the time, season, date, or circumstance, you can jump ahead of your competition.

I'm sure you have had a recent experience trying to connect with a vendor and experienced voicemail hell, no return calls, or no one available. Think Comcast, Direct TV, or many of your newer technology firms.

Years ago, we decided to begin answering our phones 24 hours a day. We don't use an answering service; it falls back to one of us, the owners to answer the phone after hours.

I'm usually the lucky owner that gets to talk to our clients after hours. Last night, one of our long-time farm clients called at 9:22 pm, he just bought a truck, was concerned it might get damaged in the storm that was brewing and wanted to make sure he had coverage.

I took care of him and eliminated any worry he had about his "new baby." He was proud of his new purchase, we chatted a few minutes, he had a need and his insurance provider was available.

Try doing that with an online company, or your traditional insurance provider. There is a reason we are growing, and there is a reason people stay with our firm.

Last night, my phone rang at 2:33 am. It was not our office number, it was a Muncie, Indiana number. It was our alarm company; the alarm had gone off at our office in Beautiful Parker City, Indiana.

The cops were going to be called to check on the situation, the caller thought the storms might have jarred the door causing the alarm to "go off," but they had to check.

He asked me for the password, and I gave him what I thought the password was, I was wrong. We went back and forth a little before he said, "Bud, it's 2:30 am and I understand you don't know your password." A password is a verification tool they use to make sure the person that answers the phone is not under duress.

At 2:33, with sleep in my eyes, I was not under duress, I was pretty groggy. My alarm guy lets me off the hook, told me they would call back if there were an issue. I didn't get a call; I think our agency is safe.

It seems to be a common theme to tell people to "go to the website" if you have service needs.

It seems that all of your customer services are available online and I'm fine with that approach, but not for our customers. Our customers, at times, want more, they want to talk to a real live human being.

Do not force your clients to listen to some cheesy voicemail greeting at their time of need. If a client needs us at 8:21 am, we answer the phone. If a client needs us at 8:21 pm, we answer the phone and if a client needs us at 2:33 am, we answer the phone.

You are only as good as your availability. If you are not available, people will go to another provider. But if you are available, understand your product and industry, your clients will struggle to leave. Make sure you are the best option in your industry.

People that want the lowest cost insurance do not call our firm. We are not a price shop. We offer a competitive product and price, but our service is our premium feature.

No matter your business, be available. Humans like to talk to others humans at a time of crisis or worry, and if you are not available, someone like us will always be there to take their call.

Congrats, Perry, on your new truck; if you had some damage last night, you know we will get you the claim managed. Thank you, Alarm Company, for calling me, waking me up from a dream in which I shall not disclose.

If you are a business owner, a sales person, or offer a service, be available or get a job that people don't need you at all times of the day or night. People count on you and shunning clients for something as silly as sleep will cost you clients and your reputation.

Our mission statement is "Find the Pain, Heal the Pain, Show the Love." We show our clients love by being available 25/8/366.

"If you love someone but rarely make yourself available to him or her that is not true love."
— **Thich Nhat Hanh**

3:07 AM – Living a Dream Life

"You know you're in love when you can't fall asleep because reality is finally better than your dreams."
— **Dr. Seuss**

3:07 am, rich dark thick coconut oil infused coffee in hand and I'm ready for the day.
In a couple of hours, I'll jump on a plane and head to my other home about 1,100 miles away.

I need to get a few things done out West before coming home for my son's wedding this coming Saturday.

I really enjoy my sleep, but as a task person, I have no problem getting up at 3:00 am. Truth is, I didn't use an alarm clock. I slept great, but woke up to check the time, 3:00 am and here I sit.

I'm guessing you are reading this on Monday morning. You probably got up at a normal time like 6:00 or maybe even 7:00 am. Congratulations on living a normal life.

I've chosen an unconventional life and getting up at the wee hours of the morning, although not normal, is a part of my existence.

Sleep is for suckers. Actually, sleep is not for suckers, sleep is very important and I got 5 hours in last night and I'll get a couple on the plan to hit my usual 7.

My life is better than any dream. I used one of my favorite quotes today, I've used it before and I'll use it again because, for me, it's the truth.

I'm in love so my dreams can never compare to my real life. I'm in love with my partner, my family, my opportunities, and my two cities.

If your life is not better than your dreams, ask yourself why. What is missing? Are you missing love? Are you not doing what you should be doing for your income? A dream life is an amazing life and for the last few years, I've been living in a dream.

I'm doing what I was meant to do and have all cylinders firing. I've got a coaching call in 6 and a half hours. I'll run that call from my condo in Denver. Having a couple of coaches has helped me both personally and professionally.

If you want to live a dream life, you might consider hiring a coach. A 3rd party that can challenge you, keep you on track, and hold you accountable.

Accountability is the key to a successful life. If you say you will do it, do it. If you fail, own it; but why fail?

Well 3:30, I need to get rocking. I've got to pack a little bag, organize my stuff and call an UBER to take me to the airport.

My dream life includes penning these darn thoughts every morning and it appears you have found these words through some cosmic connection.

Not much meat on the bone this am, but hey, it's early; my prime time writing time is 5:00 am, I'm not yet wide awake.

No matter who you are, no matter where you are, my wish for you is to achieve a dream life. I did, I do, and for me, it has made all the difference.

"You know you're in love when you can't fall asleep because reality is finally better than your dreams."
— **Dr. Seuss**

The $1000.00 Mistake, Grace, and Church

"Anyone who has never made a mistake has never tried anything new."
— **Albert Einstein**

I'm watching my Queen strip the bed. Time to head back to Indiana. I have my work; she has her work.

My work this morning consists of typing these words on this computer, packing, and heading home. My Queen has her agenda; it's always a joy watching her progress through her morning chores. She's the boss; I am the employee.

Yesterday, we got up and began working. I wrote, cleaned up email and then we worked on our condo. We organized, we put the trash by the door, and we cleaned up in anticipation of our departure.

I usually take out the trash, so yesterday, I was doing my duty, doing my work and took out the trash.

The trash consisted of 2 bags and a box. I had just helped my Queen empty the bathroom trash into a bag; it was logical to me, there would be two trash bags.

I took the trash and the box to the trash shoot. At our condominium complex, we have a trash shoot that drops the trash to the lowest level.

I dropped the trash in the shoot, returned to our condo, finished up some email, follow up, and we got ready to head to Boulder to see some family.

As we were getting ready to leave, I asked: "where is the dry cleaning?" My Queen said it was in a trash bag by the door.

I think I might have used the cuss word that we are not supposed to use. I watched as her face got contorted and my Queen said: "where is it?"

I said, "I threw it away." We both ran to the elevator, hit LF, that's Lower Floor where the trash shoot dumps into large dumpsters.

We found the dumpsters, and they were empty. About 5 minutes after I threw "the trash" down the shoot, the trash men came and took our trash. They were simply doing their job.

We lost about $1,000.00 worth of clothes. My Queen lost a couple of suits, a couple of shirts; I threw away a new blazer, a couple of nice shirts.

My Queen was not happy. The suits she lost are no longer made. They are irreplaceable. I was in the dog house.

I made a mistake, and my Queen could have spent the day angry, frustrated, and confused. But after about 30 minutes, we were laughing about my gaffe.

My Queen gave me grace.

As humans, we make mistakes. God knows I make a lot of them, but when someone errors, give grace.

Life is too damn short to be angry and upset. This week someone will make a mistake. It could be your spouse, child, or co-worker.

When they screw up, forgive them. You, yes you, have made mistakes and I guess you were given grace so return the favor.

My Queen will replace her suits on the airplane back to Indiana. I'll be gladly paying for these suits, and when I return to Colorado next week, I'll be making a run to replace my lost items.

No one got hurt, we lost material items that can be replaced. I will be buying a nice laundry bag for our future dry cleaning needs. Lesson learned, the grace was given, no blood, no foul.

It's Sunday, August 06, 2017. Live your life with style and grace. Do as much good as you can and when you make that inevitable mistake, share the story of my Queen and my $1,000.00 mistake.

We are attending church compliments of Southwest Airlines. We, along with another couple hundred people will fly 1,187 miles from Denver to Indianapolis. We will pray and watch our clergy show us how to buckle our seat belts.

We will have communion with our wine and crackers and pray together that we land safely.

The church is all around you; it's not just in those nice brick buildings on the corner of your town.

Attend your church, listen, learn, and do your rituals. One of the teachings of most churches is forgiveness. Forgive, for we all make mistakes.

Time to pack; Momma we're coming "home."

"Anyone who has never made a mistake has never tried anything new."
— **Albert Einstein**

The Adventure Gene...
"Wow, What a ride!"

"Life should not be a journey to the grave with the intention of arriving safely in a pretty and well-preserved body, but rather to skid in broadside in a cloud of smoke, thoroughly used up, totally worn out, and loudly proclaiming "Wow! What a Ride!"
— **Hunter S. Thompson**

There is this thing called the "Dunbar number." I'll let my friends at Wiki explain:

https://en.wikipedia.org/wiki/Dunbar's_numb er

Dunbar's number is a suggested cognitive limit to the number of people with whom one can maintain stable social relationships. These are relationships in which an individual knows who each person is and how each person relates to every other person.[1][2] Dunbar explained it informally as "the number of people you would not feel embarrassed about joining uninvited for a drink if you happened to bump into them in a bar."[3]

This number was first proposed in the 1990s by British anthropologist Robin Dunbar, who found a correlation between primate brain size and average social group size.[4] By using the average human brain size and extrapolating from the results of primates, he proposed that humans can comfortably maintain only 150 stable relationships.[5]

Sorry for the long explanation, but I think this is interesting and accurate. Think for a moment about your life, your family, your friends, and how many folks you actually know. Then think, how many of these folks would you call "your tribe?"

150 sounds like a big number, but as you begin adding to your list, it's actually a reasonable number of people that you can manage in your mind.

Other research that I will not bother to locate suggests that earlier man formed in groups of about the same number. As the number increased beyond 150, a few tribe's people would leave and start a new tribe.

Think back to this time. These tribes were living in the undeveloped land, full of animals, plants, and things that viewed the human as food.

This was not a time you could walk into a store and get a slab of meat or fresh veggies, this was a time of survival.

But at this time, this dawn of man, there would be an individual or group that would pack up their items and go find a new "land." A new opportunity, a new life.

This exercise has been repeated over and over in time. Our country was formed by a few folks that no longer enjoyed their "English" tribe and got on a boat for a new land.

I've lived in Indiana since I was born. I was born in Muncie, Indiana. Attended high school in Parker City, Indiana. Got married and lived for 17 years in a home 2 miles from where I grew up and then my life changed.

I moved out of my house after 17 years, found a new dwelling about 3 minutes from my ex-wife and kids home and lived another 5 years "home."

For 5 years, I lived in a loft in Farmland, Indiana. But during this time, I began exploring my adventure gene.

I started traveling. One of my first trips with my children was to Boulder, Colorado. We had other trips, but no place grabbed me like Colorado.

I started spending time in both my hometown, but also because I found a lover who lived in Indianapolis, began spending time in that city.

About 2 years ago, the pull of Colorado was too great and my partner and I hatched a plan that would allow us to set up a new tribe a few thousand miles away.

We took some of our belongings, traveled to our new plot of land and started a new life. But unlike the tribesman of earlier times, we regularly returned to our home.

We now have two tribes. We have our "home" tribe of Indiana and we have our "new" tribe in Colorado.

2 tribes, 2 jungles, 2 cultures that we must navigate on a daily basis. We now live in both Indiana and Colorado. We travel weekly to our homes doing work and life in both communities.

Jenny and I share an adventure gene. 5 years ago, I probably knew I had it, but never really used it, but today, our adventure gene is in full on mode.

I encourage you to see if you too share the adventure gene. A gene that would allow you to think to start a new tribe is a good idea.

It's not common. Moving to a new land where you know maybe one or two people and working to build your new tribe.

But I must tell you, it's given both of us energy. Instead of the travel sucking the energy out of our bodies and minds, we seem to be getting extra juice to carry on our daily activities and functions.

Our time is now compressed in two different communities. Our time is more valuable than ever, we have to work smart or we will fail.

We're getting ready to make a pretty big announcement. Our work has paid off, we have a few things happening in our new land, but also some exciting things continue to develop in our original "homeland."

Exercise your adventure gene. Most don't have it, but I'm thinking one or two of my readers have this itch to push past their tribe and go explore a new territory.

We did, we have, and for us, it has changed our life. Stop living within your Dunbar number.

There are almost 4 billion people in the world just waiting to connect with you, to hear your story, to share a drink, or glean knowledge from your travels.

Life is short. Enjoy and expand your existing tribe, but seriously think about investigating a new land, a new group of people and see if you too have that adventure gene.

"Life should not be a journey to the grave with the intention of arriving safely in a pretty and well-preserved body, but rather to skid in broadside in a cloud of smoke, thoroughly used up, totally worn out, and loudly proclaiming "Wow! What a Ride!"
— **Hunter S. Thompson**

Amateur Night Wisdom

"Always do sober what you said you'd do drunk. That will teach you to keep your mouth shut."
— **Ernest Hemingway**

Amateur night. That's what we have going on tonight. A time when people that normally don't get waxed, get waxed. And by waxed I mean plowed, wrecked, blasted, and drunk.

As a man who several times in his life has reached this pinnacle of achievement or in many cases, embarrassment, I'm writing to remind you a few things about an evening that is no different than any other. But an evening some people use as an excuse to drink away their boring, nasty ass, an excuse for a life.

If you must get plowed to enjoy your life, you might ask yourself why. Maybe it's time to have a sober New Years Eve? Maybe instead of waiting until tomorrow to go 30 days sober, you start that clock tonight.

My best New Years have been my sober New Years. Sobriety is grossly underrated in a society where booze flows like water. One thing I know is that sobriety is a super power.

Maybe tonight, you see what bringing in the New Year with clarity feels like.

But if you drink...

Eat

Sure the buzz is better on an empty stomach, but you act like an idiot. You do and say things you do not mean.

Are drunk words sober thoughts? This is a favorite quote from my Queen. People say things when drunk that they blame on the booze, but if you say it, you need to own it.

Don't explain away terrible, awful, statements made by a partner, friend, or loved one under the influence. If the words are spoken, there is some truth hidden in those characters, words, or symbols.

Eat before, during, and after your festivities and try and limit all the dumb ass things that could come out of a pie hole filled only with booze.

Act responsibly; your plans to start working on your body tomorrow (every year the same damn goal) will not last, but why start off feeling like shit.

Limit carbohydrates and sugars, focus on protein and vegetables adding a little carb to soak up that poison you so desperately want in your body.

UBER

If you get a DUI, you are an idiot.

Before UBER I understand your need to get home, not have to deal with your car tomorrow, but now with UBER, if you drive drunk or even buzzed, you are an embarrassment to your fellow human beings.

I don't think most people have figured out or realized the positive impact of our own personal driving service.

I like to make up stats on the spot so I'm going to say that drinking and driving deaths are down by 57.76% since the adoption by most of us of UBER.

A totally made up stat, but UBER has saved the lives of many loved ones and so, thank you UBER, welcome to the party. Thank you for your service.

Download the UBER app now, set it up with a credit card and never again spend the night in jail with that meth head that keeps asking you for a cigarette.

Be Joyful

2016 got a bad rap. If you think about all you accomplished this year, you had a pretty damn good year.

Before you get blasted, wasted, or sorrowful for this horrible year, take some time and write down your successes, your wins, and your most memorable moments.

Maybe the year didn't go how you wanted. Maybe one of your favorite stars overdosed on cocaine or passed after years of killing their body and mind. Maybe those events are reminders that every moment counts.

Look back with appreciation, but look forward to awe and opportunity. 2016 was good, but 2017 will be great.

Well, my last blog, muse, and thoughts for 2016. I encourage you to make changes you know you need to make to become a better human being.

Love more, give more and listen more. Appreciate mental clarity and do not overdo it. Your mind and body will thank you in the morning.

It's time we all grew up a little. I'm still the 13-year-old boy laughing at fart jokes, making fun of my friends, and playing my air guitar every time a Van Halen song comes on our Sonos. But in my 48th year around the sun, I'm giving back.

I'm going to help others. I'm going to spend the next year in service mode. Giving others what they need to live better lives. I'm going to continue to write, but offer myself to others for free.

Be safe, be kind, and be joyful. I'm off to change the world. I'm off to work out with my

Queen. I'm off to set about a day that will be no different than any other and I'm looking forward to waking tomorrow ready to take on a new year and new opportunities.

Join me, won't you?

"Always do sober what you said you'd do drunk. That will teach you to keep your mouth shut."
— **Ernest Hemingway**

Amplify Your Human Connections – Talk to Strangers

"Don't walk in front of me... I may not follow
Don't walk behind me... I may not lead
Walk beside me... just be my friend."
— **Albert Camus**

Yesterday was a great day. Many people might say yesterday was a good day, but always remember good is the enemy of great.

As you go through your life journey, you will meet fellow members of your tribe. They are all around you; they share the same values, ideas, and vision for what society could be.

My new friend Josh invited me to a meeting. I don't ask a lot of questions when a fellow tribe member asks me to join them, I simply go.

I stopped by his new office at Collaborate 317 in Greenfield, we spoke for a few minutes. It seems he and I were destined to meet. He met my Queen a couple of years ago, and through various contact points in the universe, we finally met.

After our brief chat, I met with a group of about nine people. I knew a couple of the folks, another new friend Luke, Josh, and seven others.

A painter led the meeting. His name is Harrison Painter, a newer addition to the Indiana community. Harrison recently returned after a stint in L.A., California.

The meeting was to connect fellow like-minded people. All with the same purpose of serving our fellow humans. I would guess we have all have different political perspectives, religious views, and thoughts on solutions for our current social crisis, but those thoughts and ideas were not the focus of yesterday's chat.

Yesterday was all about connecting with new ideas, learning about the other people in the room, it was not a networking meeting, it was a meeting of carefully selected individuals with a common goal.

The meeting lasted about 90 minutes, we all left better humans than before the meeting started. Keep your eye on Harrison Painter if you are in the Indianapolis area. He and his team are building something cool, and I invite you to get on his train before it leaves the station.

Find him on Facebook, connect, and maybe you might get an invite to his next Amplify meeting. I promise, connecting and attending an Amplify meeting will not be a waste of time.

I returned home, had a video meeting with some of our team. One of our insurance carriers just went through a major reorganization, we got the inside scoop and learned about how to navigate through their new organizational chart.

About 5:01, I ran to our local street taco joint and picked up 40 tacos. I returned home; my Queen had cooked some amazing food, she's the best damn skinny chef I know.

At 6:00, our home became filled with old and new friends. I'm a part of a small group that meets monthly in Indianapolis. It's a group of Smart, Accomplished, and Motivated Individuals. All business owners, all with a common goal of changing our world.

We drank, we ate, and we laughed and talked civilly about various topics including politics, business, wine, and rock and roll.

I've learned that life is about the human connection. Positive human connections can improve your life journey ten-fold.

As I looked around our courtyard, I realized that many of the people visiting our home had come into our lives in the last two years. The last two years has been an amazing time of new friendships and personal growth for my Queen and me.

Talk to strangers, connect with like-minded folks, invite them to your home, talk, listen, and learn about other people that share your passion for life.

If you don't have a passion for life, find one. Life is too short not to live with passion for positive change in our world.

We hit the bed about eleven, rather late for us, but it was worth the missed couple hours of sleep. We formed deeper connections with our friends; in the scheme of life, I'll take a deeper understanding of my fellow humans over a couple of hours of sleep.

I'm blessed, lucky, and fortunate to have found fellow tribe members in both my home towns. The people of Denver, Colorado have welcomed us like we have been a part of that community for years and our other "new" home of Indianapolis have also rolled out the welcome mat, surrounding us with another group of amazing, beautiful humans.

My words are meant to inspire. My words are meant to remind you to connect with your fellow humans. Your life will be richer, not because of money or stuff, but because of the human connections you make along your life journey.

Get up, get out, and talk to strangers. There are amazing people all around you, but first, you have to say "Hi, my name is..."

Start a conversation with a stranger and watch as your life journey takes you to places you never dreamed possible.

"Don't walk in front of me... I may not follow
Don't walk behind me... I may not lead
Walk beside me... just be my friend"
— **<u>Albert Camus</u>**

Anger Is a Poison. Let it go...

"Holding anger is a poison...It eats you from inside...We think that by hating someone we hurt them...But hatred is a curved blade...and the harm we do to others...we also do to ourselves."
— **Mitch Albom**

Are you mad? Are you angry? Let it go. No matter what has got you a little frustrated, angry, or confused, let it go.

I no longer live angrily. Agreeing instead to forgive my enemies for their transgressions. I don't hold onto any hate or wish them harm.

I've learned that bad people will have a bad life and good people will have a good life. Choose to be good and your life will follow your actions.

No matter what that person did to you, forgive them. It's hurting you much more than it's hurting them. Were they wrong? Probably, but let it go. Your anger is hurting no one, but you.

I know people that live an angry existence. They are constantly complaining, throwing blame at others, and they seem to never accept personal responsibility for their actions. I'm guessing you know this person or persons.

I don't have time for these folks and so over time, I simply remove them from my life.

Life is too damn short to live angrily. As soon as you can let the anger go, those feelings will be replaced by joy and love. It does not happen overnight, but it will happen, I speak from experience.

If you are divorced, try and get along with your former mate. There was a day when you were in love.

If you had a failed business deal, let it go. Chances are you were very good friends with that son of a bitch that caused you so much pain.

If you are going through a disagreement, don't hate, don't get angry, try and see the other person's perspective. It will help you better frame your position and you just might understand why they are a little upset as well.

Once you forgive, forget. Let it go. Stop carrying around that baggage of hate and anger and choose to use that part of your brain for personal and professional development.

You need not be friends with your former foe. I have a few folks in my life I've let go. They no longer deserve to be included in my joy-filled love of life journey.

I am surrounded by people that love, support and enjoy my perspective on life. I pick my friends and business associates carefully.

It took me a few years to understand I was in complete control of whom I let in and whom I should kick out, but if you are a human, you know who should be "in" and who should "be out" of your life.

It's Monday morning, a fresh start to a new week. Send a quick note of apology, let that individual know you no longer are upset. Let them off the hook for their thievery, gluttony, or indiscretion.

Life is too short to live angrily. It is up to you to see the good and let go of the bad. Join me, live an angry free life. I did, I do, and that has made all the difference.

"Holding anger is a poison...It eats you from inside...We think that by hating someone we hurt them...But hatred is a curved blade...and the harm we do to others...we also do to ourselves."
— **Mitch Albom**

The Angry Monday Playbook

"If you want to understand a society, take a good look at the drugs it uses. And what can this tell you about American culture? Well, look at the drugs we use. Except for pharmaceutical poison, there are essentially only two drugs that Western civilization tolerates: Caffeine from Monday to Friday to energize you enough to make you a productive member of society, and alcohol from Friday to Monday to keep you too stupid to figure out the prison that you are living in."
— **Bill Hicks**

The wind is blowing outside. She sounds angry. I wonder who pissed off the wind this morning.

Wait, it's Monday, maybe the wind doesn't like Mondays. Most people don't, but let me remind you why Monday is fifty shades of awesome.

Monday is a blank slate. Monday is a do-over of last Monday that maybe didn't go so well. Monday is the day you can make those calls that you dread making.

Those calls that you dread making, but once you are finished, you always think, "well that wasn't so bad."

Imagine just for a moment that you are in sales. It does not matter what you sell, but you are a sales person.

Now imagine yourself in front of a stranger. The stranger just realized you were a damn salesperson and begins telling you all the reasons they would never buy from you.

What do you do? How do you react? What do you say? Well, don't do anything. Don't react, don't speak, simply listen.

At some point, that person will stop throwing anger and open their mind to listen to you. Connect with that person, don't sell them anything, look for a common bond, offer them a little education about what it is you do.

Monday is like that stranger, that prospect that is telling you all the reasons that they won't buy from you.

Monday is making you feel a certain way. What is Monday trying to tell you? Most people I meet in a sales situation are defensive. They look at me, well, they look at all sales people, as trying to take something from them, but great salespeople understand that is part of the sales process.

There are times in life we need to listen and if you woke up today hating your life, your job, or this very day, why?

Listen to Monday, she's telling you something. She's whispering things you need to adjust so that next Monday you wake up with passion.

Monday is like that angry prospect that agreed to see you and then is angry about their decision.

Listen to Monday. Why do you feel the way you feel? I woke with joy. I'm off to Chicago to join a merry bunch of men doing a very cool project.

I'm working with them on this project. I will manage the risk of this merry group of men trying to change the world.

Hello Monday, I've been waiting for you.

Embrace Monday. Embrace every day with zest, joy, and love. If you are not happy, ask yourself, "why?"

Monday will speak, as will the rest of your life and it will tell you what things you need to adjust to becoming happy.

The world is yours. Don't live with fear, anger, or confusion. What is the world, what is Monday trying to tell you?

Listen. Listen to Monday, listen to all those voices, figure out a few positive steps and never wake up on a Monday feeling as you did this cold, blowing, dark day in January of 2017.

Good luck, I'm off to change the world. Join
me, won't you?

"If you want to understand a society, take a
good look at the drugs it uses. And what can
this tell you about American culture? Well, look
at the drugs we use. Except for pharmaceutical
poison, there are essentially only two drugs
that Western civilization tolerates: Caffeine
from Monday to Friday to energize you enough
to make you a productive member of society,
and alcohol from Friday to Monday to keep you
too stupid to figure out the prison that you are
living in."
— **Bill Hicks**

Are YOU TOO BUSY to take your clients call?

"Freethinkers are those who are willing to use their minds without prejudice and without fearing to understand things that clash with their own customs, privileges, or beliefs. This state of mind is not common, but it is essential for right thinking..."
— **Leo Tolstoy**

I'm sitting in beautiful Parker City, Indiana. I'm sitting in the home I where I grew up.

I think it's a luxury to be my age and still be able to sit in the home where all my childhood memories were formed. My father is sitting 10 feet away reading his newspaper.

My parents live about 2 minutes from our beautiful Parker City, Indiana office. When I have back-to-back days of appointments in Central Indiana, we now spend the night with my folks.

As we were sitting on the porch last night chatting, my sister called. My sister is buying a home in Florida. A nice home, their get-away crib and eventual winter home.

She needed insurance assistance, so I offered my service. She also needed a survey done on their property. She called 3 survey companies in her new home's area, left a message for 2 of them and got a hold of the 3rd.

She explained what she needed, the 3rd company explained their process and agreed to perform the survey.

The other two never bothered to call her back. Now "the other two" will probably call her back today, but the survey has been done, she no longer needs their services.

I'm not sure why people don't answer their phones. If you are in business, people that call you are calling for a reason.

I'm not sure the margin of a survey, but the folks in the survey business need to perform surveys to stay in business. The folks at the first two survey companies must be too busy for new clients.

We recently starting using a phone answering company. Instead of our clients calling our office direct, they call our partner company. We routed all corporate numbers through their system.

They use real live human's beings and so our clients can talk to someone every time they call our office.

The partner company answers the phone, collects some information and then sends the call to the person that is best suited for the call.

We now have team members in 4 states, 6 different locations, and so centralizing our incoming calls was a key in keeping our team connected with our clients.

Our phones are answered from 8:00 am ET to 7:00 pm and then they roll to my cell phone. If someone calls our company after hours, I'd be more than happy to try and help them. If they are calling us, they might need us.

When we opened our Denver offices, we needed a solution to have a real live human answer the phone after our Indiana offices closed. Our new partner fits that bill and then can forward the Colorado calls to one of our Colorado team members.

In today's world of email, online access, and other communication tools, there is still a segment of society that wants to talk to a human.

I've stated many times as long as I own our company we will always have a human being answer the phone.

If we ever become too busy to answer the phone, we're too damn busy. As we grow, we will constantly tweak our process and systems to allow for a real live human to answer the phone.

If you are a solo-entrepreneur, growing business, or fortune 500 company, please consider having a real live person answer your phone every time someone calls your company.

Having prospects or clients leave messages and returning their calls when you are ready and able will kill your flow of new business and ability to offer amazing customer service.

Seek out a professional company to answer your phones 24 / 7. Allow them to talk to the clients and prospects and direct the calls to the appropriate team member.

The technology is there, the price is affordable and the person that now answers the phone can be repurposed to provide another valuable service to your clients or team.

If you know a survey company in South Florida, you might want to send them a link to this little blog. They have no idea they lost a client yesterday and by the time they return the call will have lost out on any chance to gain a new client.

I seem to be writing about this topic on a regular basis. Maybe I'm getting old. I'm like the cranky guy on the porch screaming "get off my lawn." But instead, I'm screaming "answer your phone" or at least have a process set up that can connect your prospects and clients with a real live human and not a damn robot.

"Freethinkers are those who are willing to use their minds without prejudice and without fearing to understand things that clash with their own customs, privileges, or beliefs. This state of mind is not common, but it is essential

for right thinking..."
— **Leo Tolstoy**

The Artistry of Vasyl Lomachenko

"Observe the wonders as they occur around you. Don't claim them. Feel the artistry moving through and be silent."
— **Kahlil Gibran**

Sunday morning, 8:00 am, I slept in. I am finding myself doing this a little more on the weekends.

Our work weeks are getting intense, my body and mind need to rest. I'm not taking as good of care of myself as I have in the past. We are what we tolerate and I'm tolerating less than my best existence. This will soon change, but for now, I seem to be enjoying my Hunter S. Thompson type existence.

I woke up yesterday, wrote my muse, worked a couple of hours and then played guitar. I looked at my partner and claimed: "I think I'm an artist."

She said, "you are an artist."

I used my artistic powers to go to our local grocery, a couple other little neighborhood shops, and then returned home to write, relax, and play more guitar.

10 years ago, I did not write. 10 years ago, I didn't play guitar. Well, I still don't really play

guitar. I'm working on that skill daily, but I can pick enough to keep myself interested.

I wonder what skills I'll develop in the next 10 years. I'm of the mindset I can do anything. There is nothing that with practice I can't do in a functional manner.

Writing has become my personal therapy, throwing words down on paper daily. It's the first thing I do and I am constantly thinking about tomorrow's topic or idea. Imagine writing 500 to 1000 words a day, what in the hell would you say?

I consider myself a finder, a searcher for things interesting and unusual. As a child, I loved boxing. I would watch HBO boxing and see Sugar Ray Leonard and Marvelous Marvin Haggler.

When Mike Tyson came on the scene, I was a big fan. But when Tyson lost his edge, I lost interest. The last few years have not been kind the sport of boxing, but boxing will soon see a resurgence.

Do me a favor and Google Vasyl Lomachenko. They call this guy the "Matrix Fighter" because it appears he is fighting in the Matrix.

He moves like no other fighter has ever moved. He jumps around his opponents, he has only fought 8 professional fights but won 300 as an amateur.

Vasyl Lomachenko is an artist. He's taken boxing to the next level. Like Steve Jobs did with technology, Vasyl is a game changer.

Even if you do not like boxing, I highly recommend you watch a highlight reel on YouTube of this amazing 29-year-old.

Well, a pretty poor excuse for a morning blog. Not much meat here and if I can introduce a few folks to this man from the Ukraine, I'll take that as a positive impact on society.

Another introduction I can make to you, my dear reader this glorious Sunday morning is to Google the band Greta Van Fleet.

Young rockers from Michigan that just released a 4 song EP that has shades of Zeppelin, Rush, and Sabbath. Listen to Highway Tune and it just might be your soundtrack for your day.

Well, my work here is done. Time to work a couple hours setting up my next couple of weeks of appointments, connections, and try to find pain, heal pain, and show love.

Enjoy your Sunday, the sky in Denver is a brilliant blue, I think I'll take my Queen for a long urban hike today.

Get up, get out, and move.

"Observe the wonders as they occur around you. Don't claim them. Feel the artistry

moving through and be silent."
— **Kahlil Gibran**

Ashes to Ashes

"Besides the alternate universe offered by the book, the quiet space of a museum was my favorite place to go. My mom said I was an escapist at heart . . . That I preferred imaginary worlds to the real one. It's true that I've always been able to yank myself out of this world and plunge myself into another."
— **Amy Plum**

I'm sitting in my favorite place in the world. I'm sitting about 100 yards from Boulder Creek, in Boulder, Colorado.

I "found" this place about five years ago with my kids and now hang out here about every six weeks.

My question for you this morning is where is your favorite place? Where, if money, time, or energy were no issue would you choose to live, land, or visit on a regular basis?

We rolled in last night about 7:00 pm. We just returned from Ten Sleep, Wyoming.

My partner's father's final wish was that his ashes be spread in the bluffs of Ten Sleep.

There was a group of 30 of us that connected to celebrate the life of Jerry Dils.

It was a great time, it was Jerry's last wish, and I was fortunate to be a part of the event.

I've never spread someone's ashes. It was a pretty special event.

It's July 4th, and I'm heading up the side of a mountain. I'm going to hike with the love of my life and then connect with some friends later this afternoon.

Today, I'm making my public request to my family and friends that when I die, I'd like my ashes spread in Boulder Creek.

I don't plan on dying until I'm 114, so someone, anyone, please remember my final wish.

So where will your ashes be spread?

"Besides the alternate universe offered by the book, the quiet space of a museum was my favorite place to go. My mom said I was an escapist at heart . . . That I preferred imaginary worlds to the real one. It's true that I've always been able to yank myself out of this world and plunge myself into another."
— **Amy Plum**

The True Love Customer Service Approach

"If you love someone but rarely make yourself available to him or her, that is not true love."
— **Thich Nhat Hanh**

I was carrying various items in my hands; I was at a grocery store looking for my partner. She had the cart; I was on a mission to get coconut oil!

My phone rang, it was Ruby. Ruby is our phone answering company; someone was calling me on a Saturday afternoon via my office.

I answered, and it was a client that had just had a lightning strike. The lightening had hit her tree, and a limb had shot through the neighbor's roof.

I had a nice conversation and then walked over to customer service to borrow a pen   I took some information and called our team at Damage Doctors. They answer the phone when I call (thank you Mr. Dalton), James sent someone out immediately.

About an hour later, I got a call that there was no damage, the tree needed to be removed from the neighbor's roof.

I tracked down one of our tree service teams, and within that next hour they had surveyed the damage, and they had an appointment to remove the tree Monday morning.

Yesterday, Sunday, I got a text from my client, it read: "Thank you! They are coming on Monday morning to remove the limb!"

Insurance Claims do not happen Monday through Friday 8 am to 5 pm. Insurance claims happen during the evening, early mornings, and on the weekends.

I'm in the insurance business, and I'm available when needed. I don't turn my phone off when I sleep, I don't hide from clients when they need me, they bought a promise from our firm, and I help keep that promise.

Thursday night, I got a call from a client that had some water damage. I think it might have been midnight in Indiana when the claim occurred; we took care of that client as well.

I don't care what industry you find yourself working; it is of paramount importance to be available when your clients need you.

When things go wrong, people want to talk to an educated human. They don't want voice mail; they don't want to leave a message, they simply want to share their story and have someone help them figure out a solution.

Your clients do business with you because you provide answers, but not just during the old traditional office hours.

As business owners, we need to be available at all times, problem-solving, showing the love at all times of the day and night.

If you own business, answer your phone. If someone sends you an email and you won't be checking your email, give your cell phone via an auto responder. There is a good chance if someone sends you an email, they need some attention.

When my father owned our insurance agency, the world was a little different. Cell phones didn't' exist; instant human contact was a dream, not reality. But today, we have the tools and technology to stay connected to our clients, employees, and vendors every second of every day.

I encourage you to build systems that allow for your clients to connect with you at all times, not just Monday through Friday 8 to 5. If you want to test your current insurance program, call your current agency at 9:18 pm and see if real live human answers the phone.

Give them a call at 2:33 pm on a Saturday or Sunday and see if some happy shiny human picks up or you are left waiting for Monday to get the answers you need.

My promise to our clients is that we will be available. We have clients in 25 states, in multiple time zones. When they need us, we will be there. I encourage you to do the same, or one of your competitors will eventually outshine your firm and gain a new client.

Find the pain, heal the pain, show the love!

"If you love someone but rarely make yourself available to him or her, that is not true love."
— **Thich Nhat Hanh**

The Inevitability of Bad

"People aren't either wicked or noble. They're like chef's salads, with good things and bad things chopped and mixed in a vinaigrette of confusion and conflict."
— **Lemony Snicket**

We are UBER people. We UBER frequently. In the past three years, we have had approximately 250 UBER rides.

All have been awesome; all 250 have been great experiences, ending with us arriving safely at our destination.

Yesterday, that changed. We just flew back from our home in Indianapolis. We landed at Denver International Airport, we requested our UBER and were picked up by a nice young lady.

The only option that was given yesterday at the airport was UBER pool. UBER pool allows the driver to pick up others when you are in the car. We had never done an UBER pool and thought, "why not"?

The young lady picked us up, and as we were about 5 minutes from our home, she took a sharp right to pick up another rider. The only problem, she could not find the rider.

Shortly after that, another rider requested, she accepted, and we drove around another 15 minutes looking for her other rider. In her defense, we never could find that rider as well.

Our normal 30-minute commute from the airport turned into an hour drive through Denver; we had nowhere to be, so it was fine, but after 2 hours on a plane, we wanted to get home.

Finally, we arrived at our home, unpacked, and realized that we were out of wine. Unlike in Indiana, the liquor stores are open in Colorado 7 days a week, so we requested an UBER to take us to Argonaut. Argonaut is our Walmart-sized liquor and beer store that is about 5 minutes from our home.

The young man arrived, but he could not originally find us. He arrived about 10 minutes late, I could see him driving around, and he seemed to lack a sense of direction. Long story short, that UBER ride was a train wreck as well. I'm watching the map on his phone, and he made multiple errors. We finally told him how to get to our store and a few back alleys later we arrived at our destination.

No matter what you do, no matter the situation, you are going to experience "the bad" at some point. Yesterday, we had back-to-back bad UBER experiences.

We didn't get mad; we didn't' get upset, we just rolled with the less than awesome experience. If you know you are going to have a bad time, even when unexpected, I highly recommend you enjoy the journey.

Let's say you like chicken sandwiches. Most people like chicken sandwiches. In the span of 3 years, a chicken sandwich lover will eat maybe 500 chicken sandwiches. There is a great chance that one or two of those chicken sandwiches are bad.

As humans, we tend to want to talk about those one or two bad chicken sandwiches and forget the amazing culinary delights of the other 498 chicken sandwiches.

It's Monday, July 17, 2017; you might experience something bad. It might be bad service at your lunch restaurant, it might be a bad cup of coffee at your morning coffee joint, or it might be a bad UBER ride.

Instead of focusing on the "bad," realize that for things to be good or great, you have to experience the "bad." Enjoy the bad, enjoy the experience of the horrific chicken sandwich, the bad UBER driver, or the terrible customer service at your favorite lunch spot.

Our world is not perfect. Sometimes you get a bad experience, but bad experiences are not the norm. Good and great experiences are the norm and when you have that outlier of a bad experience, enjoy it. Thank the universe, your God, or that Purple Monkey Driving your Life bus for that bad experience that reminds you to be thankful for all the other great experiences.

Life is not always sunshine and puppies. It rains to remind us to appreciate the sun. It snows to remind us to appreciate spring, summer, and fall. Life is a balance of 99% great and 1% bad. Enjoy the bad, it's inevitable. We do, we did, and that, for us, has made all the difference.

"People aren't either wicked or noble. They're like chef's salads, with good things and bad things chopped and mixed together in a vinaigrette of confusion and conflict."
— **Lemony Snicket**

A Bald Woman, Friendship, and Gifts

"Friendship ... is born at the moment when one man says to another "What! You too? I thought that no one but myself . . ."
— **C.S. Lewis**

There is a bald woman in my kitchen. I met her four years ago in the Dominican Republic. She's getting coffee; she hung out with my Queen and me last night at Red Rocks. We caught the Wheels of Soul tour. I highly recommend this show.

http://tedeschitrucksband.com/

I first met "Z" at a pool in a resort. She was alone but did not lack confidence. Jenny first spotted her, pointed at her (rude, I know) and said: "I bet she has a story."

Since one of my mantras is "talk to strangers," I approached her and said, "My name is Anson, what is your story?"

She joined us in the pool, we had a beverage together and became friends. Most friends you meet on vacation, you never reconnect with, but after meeting Z, we stayed in touch.

She's been to our Indiana home, our Colorado home and will be hanging with us in Mexico in October.

She's a beautiful woman who chooses to shave her head.   It's a unique look for a unique human being. She's got a kind soul and a zest for life.

We're going hiking today. We hiked yesterday. We're going to meet another new friend in Boulder. Meeting people is what we do. Sometimes you meet folks, and there is no connection, but other times, you meet and say "you too?"

Today I encourage you to look for fellow humans from your tribe. There are all around you, but first, you might need to introduce yourself.

Talk to others, look for those that intrigue you and ask them, "So, what's your story?" Everyone has a story, and everyone loves to share their story.

There are seven billion people in this world, and your life is richer when you add new humans to your life.

As a human, I have a very limited skill set, but one of my skills is connecting with new human beings. What are your skills, maybe you struggle to talk to new people, if that is the case, there are other gifts you possess? I do not know you, but we all have gifts.

If you can understand or define your gifts, take a DISC profile, it might help you understand a little more about who you are and maybe the gifts you possess.

I know people that spend their lives in jobs that are not maximizing their gifts. I know people that spend their life with a partner that sucks the energy from their soul. Life is meant to be a journey of love and experience. You can maximize your life by tapping into your natural gifts.

It's Sunday, July 30, 2017, the end of another month. Pick a small change you can make to your life to improve your position in this world. Life is a journey of personal growth and experiences. Don't miss your chance to have your best life ever.

"Friendship ... is born at the moment when one man says to another "What! You too? I thought that no one but myself . . ."
— **C.S. Lewis**

You Are What You Tolerate – Free Yourself or Beatle It!

"I am free, no matter what rules surround me. If I find them tolerable, I tolerate them; if I find them too obnoxious, I break them. I am free because I know that I alone am morally responsible for everything I do."
— **Robert A. Heinlein**

About every few months, I write the words "you are what you tolerate." I actually have a few go-to themes including "truth over harmony," 'the power of personal responsibility," and "creating a point of difference," but today, I'd like to remind you, "You are what you tolerate."

If you don't like something, chances are you are tolerating "it" to some degree. Today, when you complain, bitch, or moan about something, ask yourself, "Am I enabling this situation?"

If something is happening in your life that you disagree with, it is incumbent upon YOU to address it or continue your ostrich toleration. You understand ostrich toleration. If you put your head in the sand long enough, the problem will go away.

But, it won't go away. It's a problem that needs your attention.

That friend that is not really a friend.
You are what you tolerate.

Your partner or mate always hiding their phone
or changing their code.
You are what you tolerate.

Your job that seems to only be getting more
cumbersome with each passing day.
You are what you tolerate.

The lumpy ass meat sack that you wear over
your finely tuned body.
My friend, you are what you tolerate.

If something is not right in your world, take a
small step today to begin fixing it. You can't fix
everything, somethings you have to agree to
"Beatle it" or let it be and simply walk away.

What is that one thing in your life that seems
out of whack? What's troubling you? What
was that thing you thought of this morning
when you first woke up?

Weights of life are carried by only those that
choose to add pressure to their life. If you are
weighed down with an issue, human, or
negative situation, you are part of the problem.

Stop tolerating bad performance.
Stop tolerating lies, mistruths, and deception.
Stop tolerating those people in your life that no
longer give you the energy they once provided.

It's time for a change and you can start with eliminating all those issues in your life that you allow to continue.

Your partner drinks too much.
Your partner no longer cares about your sexual needs.
Your kid that can't seem to get their homework done, but they just passed level 244 of that new online game.

Sound familiar?

Life is a series of choices and if your life is not all that it can or could be, it is incumbent on you to make some changes.

Figure out the issue.
Do one small thing to improve the issue.
Work on the issue, but never be willing to simply walk away.

A simple message for a simple Monday.

If your life is not what you think it should be, look in the mirror.

"I am free, no matter what rules surround me. If I find them tolerable, I tolerate them; if I find them too obnoxious, I break them. I am free because I know that I alone am morally responsible for everything I do."
— **Robert A. Heinlein**

The Cost of "Being Nice" and the Human Interaction

"We have to continually be jumping off cliffs
and developing our wings on the way down."
— **Kurt Vonnegut**

We were heading out for a bite, my friend Paul
told me about a new restaurant and so we had
to give it a shot.

If you have not been to Indianapolis lately, I
recommend a visit. According to a statistic
floated last night, there are 20 new restaurants
that have opened in the last 6 months. I'll
remind you that 87.76% of all statistics are
made up on the spot.

The dropper of said knowledge happened to be
the owner of a resort. He's in the know about
such things. But he also added very few will
actually make it.

Competition is fierce in Indy right now. New
concepts, ideas, and food choices allow for
many different culinary experiences.

We expected a wait when we arrived. We had
been hearing a few friends chat up this specific
restaurant so we wanted to see about all the
fuss.

When we entered, there was a line. It was a Thursday night, not normally a busy time, but we arrived at 7:00 and were told it would be an hour wait.

There were three young ladies at the front; the initial interaction was a little dicey. They were proud of their wait time, aloof with the attitude of "if you don't like it, leave."

We opted to stay, head to the bar and get a cocktail. As we were sipping on our drinks, my cousin, the previously mentioned resort owner was talking about success rates of restaurants.

He said owning and running a restaurant is like working on a new machine. It does take the time to work out the kinks. In his experience, it usually takes a year to get the machine humming like a well-oiled machine.

Our food was amazing, the service staff made up for the front young ladies' bitchy attitude and so we will return.

But there is a lesson in our experience for all business owners. You will not always be the new shiny object of desire. At some point, the shine wears off and you become just another restaurant.

No matter what stage of development of your business, you have to remember to be kind to your clients. Be nice, be welcoming, it costs nothing to be nice.

To put it another way, be joyful no matter the stress of a season. Be present, enjoy the moment, but remember human interactions trump interior design and food quality.

I think most people would prefer an enjoyable human interaction and average food over amazing food and average human interaction.

People matter. People matter more than anything else your business has to offer. It is you, your people, and your promises that people will remember the next time they are able to choose if they will return to your company no matter the offering.

So be nice. Remind your people to be nice. It costs nothing to be nice. Smile, engage clients and welcome them to your shop no matter if you are physical or virtual.

We recently engaged a young person to start setting some appointments for our sales people. Her job is to contact people and engage them in a conversation to see if she can uncover pain. She is looking for insurance pain and so far, so good. She's setting up some pretty good appointments, but she called me yesterday and said: "some people are just downright mean."

I laughed, "mean people are not who we want as clients, it's a good determining factor of how they might fit into our culture."

I get contacted multiple times a week from various sales people trying to sell me stuff. I'm never mean, I listen, and usually tell them I'm not interested, but usually, refer them to a friendly competitor.

So, when that young sales person reaches out, don't blow them off. Listen to them, kindly tell them you are not interested and end the call. But listen to their words, is something they are saying resonating with you?

People hate to be sold, but they love to buy. If you are buying, be nice. If you are selling, be nice. If you are the new shiny business in a community, be nice because eventually, the shine will wear off and like every other business, you'll simply be left with that one true indicator of a successful business, the human interaction.

"We have to continually be jumping off cliffs and developing our wings on the way down."
— **Kurt Vonnegut**

Stop Bitching and Start Kicking. 5 Life Rules

"They say a person needs just three things to be truly happy in this world: someone to love, something to do, and something to hope for."
— **Tom Bodett**

5 Life Rules
Be on time, in fact, be early.
If you say you will be there, be there.
If you say you will call, call.
If someone calls you, return their call.
If you are going to be even one minute late, let the person know, "I'm going to be one minute late."

I'm moving past that part of life where the majority of my time is spent in sales. I'm moving to a place in life where my main job is the personal and professional development of others.

When working with folks I hear a lot of excuses. But there are no excuses.

There are no legitimate reasons why you can't follow through on your promise.

If you say it, play it.

Successful people commit to an action and then execute that action. If you get up in the morning and say "I'm going to do X" you only succeed if you do X. If you do Y or Z, you failed. Success is predicated not just on what you do, but what you say you will do.

If you want to succeed at nothing, promise nothing.

But the person that promises nothing will have nothing. I know several people that live a below average existence because they never do anything. You know these folks, a waste of seeds and eggs.

Look around, there are people, places, and things that need attention. Do your part, it's time you, yes YOU, began participating in our world.

My neighbor's name is Bill. Another's name is Sondra. Both Bill and Sondra are a little miffed at the condition of the alley that runs behind our home.

They've been asking for some help from the department of public works, but so far, no action has been taken.

They reached out for my help. I created a one-page flyer, on the advice of Bill included some photos of the dire nature of our alley and will soon be going door to door with said flyer asking all our neighbors to do three small actions to help see that our alley is paved this spring.

When I return to Indianapolis, I'll visit with my fellow Alley Users / Livers and engage them to take a little of their time to improve our world. Some will take actions, others won't, but we will get a new alley. A few of us will do the work and everyone will benefit.

Wouldn't it be better if you were in the "I helped make that happen club" versus the "I didn't do shit club?"

Look at your world. What is in disrepair, what needs attention, what used to be bright and shiny, but now looks dull and void of life?

Small actions, small steps, little tiny group projects can change our world, but get involved and do what you will say you will do.

Follow through. Join in your local community, join in your state needs, join your fellow citizens and have an impact on your country, or your world.

Stop bitching and moaning on social media and go outside and actually do something. Your words are getting tired. Your constant belittling of ideas, people, places, and things is showing your true colors.

There are bitchers and there are kickers. Stop bitching and start kicking.

It's time to end your personal excuses and follow these 5 simple rules.

5 Life Rules

Be on time, in fact, be early.
If you say you will be there, be there.
If you say you will call, call.
If someone calls you, return their call.
If you are going to be even one minute late, let the person know, "I'm going to be one minute late."

"They say a person needs just three things to be truly happy in this world: someone to love, something to do, and something to hope for."
— **Tom Bodett**

A Black Paper on Father's Day

"When I was a boy of 14, my father was so ignorant I could hardly stand to have the old man around. But when I got to be 21, I was astonished at how much the old man had learned in seven years."
— **Mark Twain**

Why, in the business world, do we write white papers on various ideas and topics? Why not use the term black paper, or yellow paper, or red paper?

I could probably research the history of the term, but I think I shall just blame it on privileged white men. They seem to get the blame for everything. Oh hell, let me do a little research.

It's times like these, I turn to my friends at Wikipedia. And the real reason we use the term white paper is:

*"A **white paper** is an authoritative report or guide that informs readers concisely about a complex issue and presents the issuing body's <u>philosophy</u> on the matter. It is meant to help readers understand an issue, solve a problem, or make a decision.*

The initial British term concerning a type of government-issued document has proliferated—taking a somewhat new

97

meaning in business. In business, a white paper is closer to a form of marketing presentation, a tool meant to persuade customers and partners and promote a product or viewpoint.[1][2][3] *White papers may be considered* gray literature*."*

So there you have it, the history of the term white paper. From now on, I will not produce white papers. I shall produce black papers.

My ideas and thoughts seem to buck the usually accepted narrative, so it makes sense that my diatribes on various topics and ideas would not have the same name as others writing similar summaries of ideas.

I think I'll write a black paper on white papers.

I'm surprised with the extreme focus on race that no one has ever held this up as an example of racism.

I view race as I do the color of one's hair. To say all blondes act or live a certain way is ignorant and ridiculous.

Instead of judging folks on the color of their skin, hair color, or another trait I view people as individuals. There are good white people and there are bad white people. There are good black people and bad black people. There are good blondes and bad blondes, and there are good gingers and bad gingers.

I think I might write a Ginger Paper.

It's Father's Day, I should probably write about my father or what it means to be a father or something father-like, but in bucking the normal trend of what I should write about I thought I'd do a little tongue and cheek diddy about white papers.

It's Fathers Day, why are you reading a blog from some white guy sitting on a cheeseburger bean bag chair in Colorado?

Get up, go spend time with your father or if your father is passed, remember the great times and the lessons he taught you.

My father is about 1,100 miles away, my children are also 1,100 miles away, so this is my way of deflecting not spending Father's Day with my father.

I shall spend my day in the mountains with my mate, my partner, my lover, my guiding light. I'll think about my father, my children and the love I have for all.

My partner lost her dad in October. She's not sad today. She was just talking about people that are overly sad on Father's Day at the passing of their father.

Her father was a great man who raised great kids, built an amazing company, and left a legacy in a community in East Central Indiana.

Instead of sadness, my partner is choosing to celebrate the memory of her father. I think my partner could write a great black paper on focusing on the positive aspects of the loss of one's father.

All humans die; you can choose to be sad or choose to look at all the awesome and amazing things your deceased father did.

My dad is 77, he's old, but I think he has another 20 or so years to go before he checks out. When he dies, I'll be sad, but without him, there is no me, and without me, there are no children.

My dad reads my stuff every day, he might have a little tear in his eye right this very moment. He seems to get emotional these days, so Dad, know today as I'm climbing that mountain, I'll be thinking of you, celebrating the man you taught me to be.

I'll think about Jenny's father and the lessons he taught me, I'll think of all the men in my life that gave me an appreciation for work, life, and happiness.

Seriously, you are still reading this white guy rant on black papers and fathers? Put your phone, laptop, or tablet down and go outside.

It's a beautiful June day. Celebrate your father's teachings, celebrate the creation, and celebrate the choice you have to write white, black, or ginger papers.

I need to call my Dad, enjoy your day and thanks for hopefully sharing a little smile with me this beautiful morning.

It's time to go do life.

"When I was a boy of 14, my father was so ignorant I could hardly stand to have the old man around. But when I got to be 21, I was astonished at how much the old man had learned in seven years."
— **Mark Twain**

Beautiful Parker City, Indiana and Monroe Central High School

"So many people walk around with a meaningless life. They seem half-asleep, even when they're busy doing things they think are important. This is because they're chasing the wrong things. The way you get meaning into your life is to devote yourself to loving others, devote yourself to your community around you, and devote yourself to creating something that gives you purpose and meaning."
— **Mitch Albom** (**Tuesdays with Morrie**)

I grew up in a little town in Indiana called Beautiful Parker City, Indiana. It's a town of about 1,300 people; think of the T.V. show Mayberry, and you can get an idea of my childhood.

You know everyone in Beautiful Parker City, Indiana and well, everyone knows you.   It was an amazing place to grow up, we had and still do have the best little league park in America.

Beautiful Parker City, Indiana is home to the legendary Jerry's Dairy Freezer. Think Dairy Queen, but with many more options and magical cherry cokes.

Growing up, we had a bank, but with time, the bank, like most small-town banks, shut down forcing us to drive the long 4-mile drive to our sister city, Farmland, Indiana. Yes, our sister city is named Farmland, Indiana. There was once a fierce rivalry between the citizens of Beautiful Parker City and Farmland, but in the early 70's the school systems were consolidated, and both communities became part of the Monroe Central School Corporation.

I graduated from Monroe Central. When I graduated, I was 33 in my class of 99. Top third and I have no idea how I finished so high. I was not a good student. I was a little bored in high school, choosing to spend my time drinking and smoking instead of hitting the books. I didn't learn to hit the books until college.

My children went to Monroe Central High School. I bought a small farm about 3 minutes from the school and was married 17 years, living in that farm house, while my kids attended my alma mater.

On Saturday, August 12th, Monroe Central is having a community day to celebrate the positive changes that have occurred in our community.

The driving force behind this Community Day event is a young man by the name of Ron Braun. Ron, like me, is a local boy. He is the head of our cross-country team, and he has taken our cross-country program from a small band of average runners to a powerhouse in the state.

Ron has worked with the other coaches and the administration to create an event that is as wholesome as apple pie and Chevrolet.

On Saturday, August, 12th, at 3:01 pm, there will be a car show with 100 plus cars. There will be bands, all local talent from both Beautiful Parker City and Farmland, Indiana. There will be burgers, brats, and corn on the cob. There will be a "corn hole" tournament. There will be various activities for any aged human from 1 year old to 99 years old.

At dusk, the cross country 3.2-mile track will be lit with luminaries and the entire mass of humanity will walk our newly designed cross country course.

Parker City is named Beautiful Parker City for one reason, the people. It is full of hard working and dedicated people that truly believe that it is the greatest place on earth.

Our Superintendent, a young man by the name of Adrian Moulton, was born next to my childhood home and is a sharp young leader that, I'm betting, will retire from our school system after many years of leadership. His parents were both teachers in our school system. After college, he came home to lead his former high school.

Another young man of note is Kyle Parkison. Kyle grew up about 200 yards from the school, attended Ball State and was hired as our school's first professional athletic trainer. Kyle or K.P. is a well-known former student that will impact the lives of many young people attending Monroe Central.

Growing up, Monroe Central didn't have a football team, but about 15 years ago a group of parents banded together and pushed for a football team. It was a divisive topic that divided the community, but we eventually launched a football program, and today our football team is one of the best 2A (small school) programs in the state of Indiana. Our coach, "Coach Ho" has coached some of the best NFL talents in the game today.

Our football team has been a draw from other local school systems, bringing kids from other local schools that do not have a football program.

Justin Ulom leads our basketball team. Justin is not a local, not yet anyway. He played in a state championship game when he was in high school and brought that winning attitude to our school. Last year, we were ranked in the top 10 most of the year and looking at our prospects for this year's team, we will be ranked again. Someday Monroe Central will win a state championship. You heard it here first.

I now live in Indianapolis, Indiana, and Denver, Colorado, but we still maintain an office in Beautiful Parker City. Our team is made up of many local people that attended high school with yours truly. Our team, most educated through our Monroe Central High

School System has a strong work ethic and an appreciation for our little town.

As our company grows, we will continue to invest in our headquarters, hiring other local rock stars to help us grow our firm. As a company, we are committed to our little town.

If you ever get to Indiana, visit Beautiful Parker City, Indiana. Take a tour of "our" town, look at the beautiful homes, the nice streets, and the ball park. Grab an ice cream, slush, or cherry coke at Jerry's Dairy Freezer and check out our school system.

As other area schools are being taken over by the state for financial recklessness, teachers are leaving in droves; our little rural school continues to grow our footprint. Our athletic teams have strong leadership as does our school board. Keep your eye on Beautiful Parker City, Indiana and Monroe Central High School. It's an amazing community that continues to churn out amazing leaders that are spread all over the world.

August 12th will be an amazing event. If you are close, attend the event. If you want to see the power of a small community, it will be wildly on display starting at 3:01 pm at Monroe Central High School.

"So many people walk around with a meaningless life. They seem half-asleep, even when they're busy doing things they think are important. This is because they're chasing the

wrong things. The way you get meaning into
your life is to devote yourself to loving others,
devote yourself to your community around you,
and devote yourself to creating something that
gives you purpose and meaning."
— **Mitch Albom** (**Tuesdays with Morrie**)

Living Broken

"And then I felt sad because I realized that once people are broken in certain ways, they can't ever be fixed, and this is something nobody ever tells you when you are young and it never fails to surprise you as you grow older as you see the people in your life break one by one. You wonder when your turn is going to be, or if it's already happened."
— **Douglas Coupland**

If you are reading these words you are probably broken. Maybe you know, maybe you are blind to this fact, but if you have lived a life worth living, at some point, you "broke."

If you are broken, there is a good chance that you can't be fixed. But don't be sad, embrace your broken self.

In every life, there are things that go right and things that go wrong. We are human and thus we make mistakes. These mistakes have a tendency to pile up and eventually break us from who we were to who we are.

It's OK to be broken. I could make a case that until you break, you are a caterpillar and only until you are broken do you become a butterfly.

Maybe you are breaking right now. Maybe your life is in such a state that you can't see a way out of your current situation, but that's when life gets interesting.

When one finds themselves in a position of no hope, looking around at your fellow broken humans can give hope. We, humans, are resilient and when life gets rough, we have multiple examples that point to the beauty of the broken life.

So, dear friend, my dear reader, know that at some point you will break, but also know there is a good chance you are already broken.

The man or woman you are today is not who you were 10 years ago and the person you will become in 10 years is a person that is very different than who you appear to be today.

We break many times in life and through breaking, we become stronger, more experienced, and enlightened about our true self.

Embrace your broken self. Think about how damn broken you actually are and thank God, the Universe, or that Purple Monkey Driving the Bus for your scars and wounds.

All humans break and most can't be fixed and that is part of the beauty of life.

"And then I felt sad because I realized that once people are broken in certain ways, they can't ever be fixed, and this is something nobody ever tells you when you are young and it never fails to surprise you as you grow older as you see the people in your life break one by one. You wonder when your turn is going to be, or if it's already happened."
— **Douglas Coupland**

Is Google Broken? The Truth about Coconut Oil and the KETO Lifestyle

"To seek truth requires one to ask the right questions. Those void of truth never asks about anything because their ego and arrogance prevent them from doing so.
— **Suzy Kassem**

If you have a question, there is an answer. Not only that, it's probably 99% accurate.

We were working yesterday on an account. We were doing some research on a competitive carrier, looking up their best rating; trying to understand the who and what we were competing against.

There was a term used that both my partner didn't understand. She looked at me and said, "I'll call Rick" our insurance lawyer guru, and I said, "I'll figure it out."

Within 30 seconds and a much-focused Google search, we had our answer.

Today, there are no more unanswered questions.

If you have a question, Google it. You have Google on your phone. There have been times where someone will ask me a question about a process, idea, or concept and my sarcastic response "Is Google Broken?"

We live in a time of wonder. We live in a time of amazement where every question you can think has already been thought and the answer is in your hands.

Now, I write for the common men and women of the world. I do not write for scientists, if you are a scientist, please understand, I'm not talking about the mechanics of black matter or about the Hadron Collider's next amazing discovery.

I'm talking about everyday personal, business, and common sense questions.

Also, do me a favor and don't just be a headline consumer. Put context around everything you read. Let me give you an example.

The other day, the American Heart Association made news with this story:

https://www.usatoday.com/story/news/nation-now/2017/06/16/coconut-oil-isnt-healthy-its-never-been-healthy/402719001/

I drink coconut oil daily, have for the last year of my life. I use it to cook and our roommate in Colorado uses it on her entire body. I've made no secret of our use and passion of coconut oil.

When the article was published, many of my friends sent me this article and said: "read this…"

I'm a little sensitive about my diet and lifestyle. I switched to a KETO based lifestyle over a year ago and have experienced amazing health benefits, greater energy, and can now control my weight like never before.

I eat like a king and can manage my 6-foot 1-inch frame between 165 and 170 pounds with no problem. I have total control of my weight. I actually got down to 159 pounds before my Queen said, "gain some weight." It was no problem gaining the weight back and now I live at my "fighting weight."

I'm not alone, my Queen, and many of my friends who have tried and stuck with the program had had similar results. If you want to learn more about our KETO lifestyle, click here:

https://www.reddit.com/r/keto/wiki/keto_in_a_nutshell

What I have discovered over the past few years is that sometimes the data we are fed is not that accurate.   Obesity rates in the United States have exploded since the 1980's when the new "food pyramid" was released.

It's heavy on grains and views sugar as empty calories. If one follows this nutritional template, they will become obese. That is not a blanket statement but if a person follows the traditional food pyramid there is a very good chance, they will not be able to control their weight. Look around, people are bigger than ever before, but my opinion and the opinion of many healthy fit folks is that it's not a lack of exercise, although exercise is very important, it's the food offerings and what various health organizations like the American Heart Association push as "their agenda."

To counter the article, to show that maybe the American Heart Association, the government controlled agency that has an agenda to push their dietary guidelines, enter the company Onnit.

Onnit is a human health optimization company.

https://www.onnit.com/what-is-onnit/

They have facts, ideas, and proof that our current dietary government recommendations are a tad flawed. They release this article to debunk the American Heart Associations "fake news" report. I should also point out they sell coconut oil.

If you are concerned about coconut oil, read this:

https://www.onnit.com/academy/the-truth-about-coconut-oil/

My point is that we live in 2 competing realities. You can believe any narrative, but when you read an article or worse, a headline, ask yourself, "does that make sense?"

Before sharing the news with others, please do your research. There is a lot of bad news, fake news, trying to get society to move in a particular direction, but there are white knights that have the real story.

Who is publishing the article, what is their agenda, why might they give misleading facts?

As I stated earlier, we live in a time of wonder and amazement, but we have to be careful with our consumption of various news stories and data.

Don't just read the headlines; read the damn article. For shits and grins, read a counter article (there is always a counter article) and determine which reality you will choose to believe.

We are starting to see a major crack forming in the news produced by some of our major stalwarts of data. Old media has been caught not once, but several times creating a narrative that has been later been debunked.

Many of these stories are political, but with time the truth always comes out. Don't be so quick to rush to judgment when you hear a sensational news story. If it fits your narrative, fine, but read the damn article!

Google is NOT broken, but depending on how you use it and the depth of your search and understanding, you could be living life using flawed or skewed data.

Slow down, read, compare, and think. What does your gut tell you? Connect with similar and likeminded folks and compare your notes about life, love, sex, and diet.

But also hang out with the opposition, find out where their ideas, thoughts, and passions are derived.

My opinions are based on my personal experience and testing of various diets, exercise programs, and lifestyles.

At 48, I'm having the time of my life. Life is amazing, wondrous, challenging, and enriching. I don't see the darkness, I live in the light.

Join me, do your research, don't be a headline consumer, live your life based on real accurate data and when you have a question, simply Google it and pick the answer that you can both internally and externally justify.

"To seek truth requires one to ask the right questions. Those void of truth never asks about anything because their ego and arrogance prevent them from doing so.
— **Suzy Kassem**

Anything Can Be

"Listen to the mustn't, child. Listen to the don'ts. Listen to the shouldn'ts, the impossibles, the won'ts. Listen to the never haves, then listen close to me... Anything can happen, child. Anything can be."
— **Shel Silverstein**

As children, we are taught that anything is possible. As we age, we learn there is a reality in place that limits who we are and what we can do.

But this morning, I'd like to challenge you to think like you did as a child. Anything you can dream can become a reality.

About 90% of the people that read that last couple of lines just quit reading. Those of you that have continued, the seekers, here's the message.

Nothing is stopping you from achieving anything and everything you desire.

If you can think of a roadblock, there is a way over, under, around, or through that very road block.

No matter your education, color, creed, sexual preference, or current station in life, you, yes you, can be or do anything you can dream.

But be careful what you dream, it might just become a reality.

So, dear reader, what is your dream? What is that thing that you want to do that you think is not impossible at this stage in life?

Where is that place you would love to visit or maybe even live?

Who is that person that you want to spend the rest of your days on this planet? What do they look like, what do they feel like, and what does that person need to have to be your partner?

The only limiting factor in life is you. If you think you can't, you are right. If you think you can, you will find a way.

I speak from experience. I no longer let life's perceived limitations stop me from achieving any goal I set.

If I want to climb a mountain, I'm going to climb a mountain.

If I want to have a home on the beach, I'll have a home on a beach.

If I want to change the world, I will change the world.

The world needs you, your ideas, and your will to change all that is wrong or perceived right. There is a lot in this world that we accept as fact when, in fact, no one has ever bothered to push the limits and test the boundaries of what is possible.

You have ideas, you have thoughts, and you have things in your head that are unique to you. No other human has your thoughts, but yet you keep them hidden. You keep those ideas, those aspirations secret for fear that if you tell others, they might not believe.

Any radical idea will come with folks that do not believe. The more that do not believe in your dream, the more fuel you get to achieve your dream.

If your dream is to get a job at "The Walmart," no one will stand in your way.

But if your dream is to start a company, most people you know will point to your past failures to prove you cannot start a business, you are a failure.

But those past failures have positioned you for success. If you have not failed, you will. Maybe your dream is flawed, maybe there are things you have failed to calculate to make your dream a reality.

Only with action towards your dream will you realize your errors. Once your errors are realized, you can adjust your plan and your actions to overcome your dream.

What is your dream and why are you not taking just a little action today to make that dream a reality?

Do not listen to those that have "sense" that tell you all the reasons you can't do what you think you can do.

There are those of us that believe that anything is possible. There is a breed of men and women that will not laugh but support, and help you connect with your dream no matter how big or silly that dream sounds.

Today, this is your wake-up call. Stop living the life you have and start living the life you want.

Anything can be.

"Listen to the mustn't, child. Listen to the don'ts. Listen to the shouldn'ts, the impossibles, the won'ts. Listen to the never haves, then listen close to me... Anything can happen, child. Anything can be."
— **Shel Silverstein**

Cancer and Thunderstorms

"Whenever you read a cancer booklet or website or whatever, they always list depression among the side effects of cancer. But, in fact, depression is not a side effect of cancer. Depression is a side effect of dying."
— **John Green** (**The Fault in Our Stars**)

I had an amazing night with my Queen. It was just she and I, a little food, a little wine, and conversation.

We sat on the porch; we laughed, we talked, we laughed some more. Life is pretty amazing when you are in love.

Earlier this week, we had a little disagreement. I thought X, she thought Y and we bantered a little before concluding. We went with XY if you were wondering.

We talked about that situation, how it was a thunderstorm, a quick brief bout of lightning, thunder, and some rain. But then it was gone. We don't let conflict last, we have it, it's natural, then let it go. Life is too damn short to argue and fuss when there is so much amazing stuff going on in our world.

I think most people live their life in cloudy days. No sun, just clouds, never seeing the light of the sun, just plodding along, never getting their required dose of Vitamin D.

We live in the sun; we live in the bright light of life always looking for that next adventure.

We learned last week that my Queen has cancer. Skin cancer, it seems we may have spent too much time in the actual sun, not my analogous sun.

Unlike most, we have not shared that issue. Well, until now. We are not worried, and it's a little issue that we will deal with together. I've done cancer before; cancer is a sissy.

My ex-wife had breast cancer; she's a vibrant, beautiful woman with an amazing life. Cancer didn't beat Jodi, Jodi beat cancer.

We will be going to a doctor in a few weeks to get treatment, she will be down a few days, but my Queen is tough, she will bounce back.

I guess cancer might be another thunderstorm, but we are tackling it together. I'm sure I'll have a thunderstorm soon, and my Queen will help me battle whatever comes my way.

Life is not always sunshine and puppies. There is cancer, there is sickness, and there is death. But there are so many amazing-awesome-beautiful parts of life that we choose to focus on the latter.

My Queen's cancer is just another reminder to us to focus on the positive. Focus on the great things in our life.

It's Friday, August 04, 2017. It's going to be an amazing day. Instead of focusing on the clouds, look for the sun. It's up there, beyond the clouds and even when you can't see it, you must believe it is there.

The next few months will be a time of toil and struggle, but we are ready. We are ready for the battle; we are not alone. Cancer is a part of life, and it's not the end of the world.

Cancer, for us, is just another cloudy day, but we know the sun is shining brightly and soon, will be shining again.

"Whenever you read a cancer booklet or website or whatever, they always list depression among the side effects of cancer. But, in fact, depression is not a side effect of cancer. Depression is a side effect of dying."
— **John Green** (**The Fault in Our Stars**)

Your Cell Phone Battery % Controls Your Current Mood

I'm flying at 30,000 feet somewhere over the United States of America. I have no scientific basis for what I'm purposing, but I think that there is a direct correlation between your cell phone battery charged percentage and your present mood.

When you wake up, most of us have charged our phones during the evening. We wake up with 100%, a green battery, we wake up with full power.

But as the day passes, we go from green to yellow to red. That process is much like the process most of us experience during our work days.

So, do me a favor, keep your phone charged. When you charge your phone, charge yourself. Whenever you see your phone battery light get yellow, allow it to be a reminder to you that you and your phone need to charge.

Plug in your phone and grab a water. Grab a healthy snack like nuts, or seeds, and enjoy and savor the pure crisp taste of cold water and some salty almonds or sunflower seeds.

Use your cell phone battery life to help remind you that you, like your phone, need juice. You need rest, time to clear your mind from all the clutter that you call life.

When you charge your phone, try and not look at it. Let it charge and focus on yourself. Think about something happy, don't worry about things you cannot control.

If you must look at your phone, save a few favorite photos in your favorites and remember those awesome times you have had with your family and friends.

One more thing, it has occurred to me over this past weekend, that people try and make other people's problems their problems.

Stop getting involved in others people's sad plights. There are millions of happy and shiny people all around. If you are hanging out with someone full of drama or is trying to make their problems your problem, kick them out of your life.

So, be like me and let your cell phone battery life be a little guide. And eliminate the drama causing folks from your life.

We did, we do, and for us, it has made all the difference. Enjoy the journey.

The Secret to Changing EVERYTHING!

"Everyone thinks of changing the world, but no one thinks of changing himself."
— **Leo Tolstoy**

5:21 am, coconut infused coffee in hand. There is a slide show of some photos from a recent hike bouncing around on the TV and the fireplace is making my writing chair toasty warm.

It's almost March. How are those New Year's Resolutions? Did you come out of the gate strong only to fail in week 2 or 3?

Are you still going to the gym or did you realize that you didn't have enough time? Are you managing your nutrition? How's that "I'm going to stop drinking so much" goal going for you?

Most people fail when setting goals. They try too damn hard, they set unrealistic goals and then when they don't achieve their desired result, they quit.

If you want to change, start small. I have a friend; his name is Joe. Joe is a coach. Joe was coaching Sally and Sally wanted to change. But Sally kept failing.

Sally wanted to feel better, but her life didn't allow her time to "work out." Sally had this dream that in order to get fit, she had to join a gym.

Joe worked with Sally and asked how she spent her evenings. Sally enjoyed watching TV. Joe and Sally made a deal.

Every night for a week, Sally would simply stand up during every TV commercial.

After a week of standing up just a few minutes at a time, Sally started getting a little more energy.

Over time, Sally began walking. Today, Sally walks daily, is in the best shape of her life and found a way to work out from home to help tone her body.

Sally needed to change, and she started her change standing for 2 minutes.

I was doing a little coaching with an employee yesterday. I was working with one of our younger team members on setting expectations.

When we set expectations, it's important that we are reasonable with our goals. My young team member sends me her schedule every morning.

She had some pretty audacious goals. She was going to make 25 prospecting calls in an hour.

I reached out to her after her first hour and asked: "how many calls did you make?" She said, "not 25."

My young team member set a goal, failed to achieve it and thus her day started with a big fat fail.

Failure sucks. But she didn't actually fail, she actually made 15 prospecting calls.

Had she set her goal at 12 prospecting calls, she would have over-achieved. One key to change is setting reasonable goals and expectations.

In working with my team, I always try and get them to set small achievable goals. If you set a goal and fail, you feel bad. It's normal; so why not set a goal that you can achieve?

When you start to change, don't go overboard. Don't suddenly say, I'm going to get in shape and I'm going to go to the gym 5 days a week.

If you are not going to a gym currently, you will never make it 5 days. Instead of making some huge goal that will ultimately lead to failure, set a small goal.

If you want to get in shape, start with a small goal. Be like Sally and start standing for 2 minutes or walk for 10 minutes around your house.

The key to getting your body in shape is simply to move. You don't need to go to a gym, you simply need to move.

Do you want to change? Then begin by making very small changes. Look long term. We, humans, like to look short term and that's why most of us fail. We tend to live in the day and not the week or the month.

If you want to change, begin by writing down the habit or activity you are committed to change. Then make small adjustments to that habit or activity.

If you look at a pile of work and think, I can't get that done. I don't have time. Simply split the stack of work into 3 or 5 piles. Work through each pile and every time you finish a pile, take a break. Reward yourself for your accomplishment.

So, 3 major things you must remember when initiating change in your life.

1. Look long-term, true change happens over weeks and months, not days.
2. Start small. Pick a goal that you know you can do. Then gradually increase that goal weekly adding just a little more "work" to that goal.
3. Reward yourself when you hit your goal. If you set goals you can achieve, you will gain satisfaction and begin getting the positive feedback you need to continue on your path to change.

Every morning, my Queen and I do 4 minutes of planks and 25 pushups. When we started, we started with 30 seconds of planks and then added a little time each week.

We didn't start with 25 pushups, we started with 10 and then gradually added a push-up or two each week.

Our workout takes about 8 minutes, add to that our daily walk and we are both in pretty damn good shape.

We don't hang out in a gym, we don't do cross fit, we don't participate in triathlons, we simply made a little movement and a minor exercise a part of our daily routine.

Pick one thing you would like to change about yourself. Maybe it's your weight, maybe it is your booze consumption, maybe it's your relationship with your significant other.

What can you begin doing today to have a positive impact on that area of your life?

Look long term, but think small. Make small changes and over time those small changes will begin to compound and provide you the sense of accomplishment to increase your goals.

Personal and professional growth happens only when we begin to change who we are and what we do.

I wish you the best of luck. I hope my words resonated with you this morning. I'm off to change the world. Join me, won't you?

"Everyone thinks of changing the world, but no one thinks of changing himself."
— **Leo Tolstoy**

Cheese and Rice – The Story of an Amish Knight Lover

"Whether a man is a legend or not is decided by history, not fortune tellers."
— **Amish Tripathi**

I drove up to see an old friend yesterday. He was in the hospital. He's battling brain cancer. I first met my friend 25 or so years ago. My ex-wife and I would buy homes, flip them, and sell them.

He was a contractor, he was and is Amish and will be, for me, a legend in my life.

John connected with me in our first visit. I was heading down to the Daytona 500, he was a big NASCAR fan, and he was intrigued that I was actually going to the race. His dream was to go to the Daytona 500. I later learned John had many dreams.

I returned from that race and started a long friendship with my friend from "another culture."

When I returned, John and his wife Ann had our family to their home. During my first visit, John was taking me a tour of his home when he showed me his "special room."

His special room consisted of a shrine to Indiana Basketball. There were posters, statistics, and other "IU" memorabilia hanging or sitting in the room. At this time, Bobby Knight was the King and John loved Bobby Knight.

I asked John if he had ever attended a game at IU, he wryly smiled, "no probably not possible." You see, John typically travels by buggy. Occasionally, he has a driver that takes him to his construction jobs, but he is not in a position to get to a city 3 hours away from his home.

A few months later, IU basketball season was in full swing. I called a friend that lived close to John. A fellow insurance agent that is now a state congressman and one day will be the governor of our fine state, but that's another story for another day.

I asked my insurance agent friend, a big Purdue fan to pick up my friend and bring him down to Muncie where we could connect with 10 or so other men and head to "the Mecca."

My friend, not overly happy that he had to go to the enemy lines, did me a favor and picked up John. We met, had a couple of beers, ate some wings, and headed to the game.

When we arrived, we found ourselves in the upper section of Assembly Hall. After a few minutes, John asked if we could simply go touch the floor. To him, this was a sacred place.

I said: "follow me." He did and we walked down on the floor. We sat courtside and as we sat down he asked, "can we get in trouble?" I replied, "just follow my lead."

We sat on the first row of the student section, it was winter break, the kids were gone, and there were plenty of seats.

John sat bright-eyed and repeatedly said, "Well Cheese and Rice!" and then pointed to the various former players in the crowd. Damon Baily was there as were many former standout players and John knew them and their stats from when they played.

John Cougar was about 20 feet away, but John didn't know John Cougar, he was more interested in the officials of the game whom he knew every name and how they might call the game.

John is and was a student of sports. He read the papers every morning gleaning little details about his favorite team. In addition to IU, he as a huge fan of the Miami Dolphins and New York Yankees. We had many conversations about how "my Colts" would kill "his Dolphins." Most of the time I was right, but when the Dolphins beat my Colts, I could expect a call from John on a borrowed cell phone.

John has said his visit to IU was one of the best days of his life, but this was not the last time he would connect with Indiana Basketball.

A few years later, John was diagnosed with brain cancer. He took his chemo treatments in Bloomington and when the nurses learned he was a fan, one of them organized a trip for him and his family to attend an IU practice.

By this time, Tom Crean was the coach and Coach Crean allowed John to join a practice with the team. John, my Amish friend, shot hoops with the players and walked on that same court that caused him to say "cheese and rice" all those years ago.

This past Saturday my son got married and midway through the reception my old friend walked in. He along with his 6 children, his wife, and 2 other young men that were sweet on his daughters joined our celebration.

As he walked in, I jumped up and gave him a big hug. He said, "when I got the invitation, I told my wife I was going to make sure I stayed alive to make it to the wedding."

He did, we caught up, and after an hour or so he had to head back to a local hotel. He was taking his family to the Indianapolis Zoo the next day.

John's time is short, after a couple of appointments, I drove to see my old friend. It was a few hours from my new home, but I fear John does not have much time left.

I pulled into his home, his two daughters were in the yard as I pulled up. I asked, "is your papa home?" The younger of the two frowned, "Nope, he's in the hospital."

I shared her frown, "hopefully," she said, "he will come home tonight."

I don't think I'll see my friend again. His time is short, but I learned much from John and his family. I went to an Amish wedding, spent a few nights at his home and as the only "English" person in at the gathering, learned about the culture and life of my friends.

John and I might have been from different planets, but we formed a bond. As I look around the world, we seem to be at a place where people that are different are shunned, not embraced, or chided for their different views.

Instead of focusing on our differences, I learned that we all have common interests and bonds. If we choose to focus on those commonalities instead of our differences, life is much richer.

Stop looking at others as different and start looking for those common bonds. I did, I do, and for me, that has made all the difference.

My life is better because I met John. I'm going to miss my friend, but know that I'm a better man for getting to experience "cheese and rice."

"Whether a man is a legend or not is decided by history, not fortune tellers."
— **Amish Tripathi**

The Sinister Issue of Children with High Blood Pressure.   Are Advertisers Influencing Some News Outlets?

"My mom's a doctor, but because she came from India and then Africa, where childhood obesity was not a problem, she put no premium on having skinny kids. In fact, she and my dad didn't mind having a chubby daughter. Part of me wonders if it even made them feel a little prosperous, like *Have you seen our overweight Indian child? Do you know how statistically rare this is?*"
— **Mindy Kaling**

When in Indianapolis, we usually head over to Mr. Tequila, a Mexican joint one block from our home. Last night I cooked, so we headed over for some fajitas.

We always sit at the bar and watch the soccer games on the bar TV. I think there is a rule that if you own and operate a Mexican restaurant, you have to purchase the soccer package and play it on a continuous loop.

But last night something weird happened, NBC News with Lester Holt was featured on the TV in front of our bar stools. I think everything happens for a reason and so I watched that evening news.

The first things I noticed was that two out of every three commercials were for some pharmaceutical drug. You know the ones that cure one little irritant but provide the user with a loose stool, death, or a host of other nasty side effects.

It got to be a comedy show; there were drugs for things I didn't know were a thing. But soon the news returned, and the drug commercials were over.

Lester introduced a segment on the growing issue of kids with high blood pressure. I watched as several doctors were interviewed about the new issue of childhood high blood pressure.

Various kids were shown getting their blood pressure checked; the message was simple, this is a growing issue. Mothers were interviewed, most did not seem educated on proper nutrition. If Mom does not know how to eat, I am pretty sure the kids don't get magic knowledge on proper nutrition.

I thought, "Kids have high blood pressure because they sit in basements and play video games." Kids have high blood pressure because the dietary guidelines we were taught as kids and then used to raise our children were based on flawed data.

Look around, many of the kids today are a little plump. Not all, don't get your back hair up, but kids today that are not athletes seem to be carrying a little more weight than in past generations.

I saw an article on our local school football team; the front line had a couple of players over 300 pounds. Even our athletes are turning their healthy bodies into massive machines that might not prove beneficial for their long-term health.

But here's the kicker, the story was about the kids and their need for, wait for it. Drugs, kids need drugs to combat the growing issue of high blood pressure.

I am not a doctor, but with a little common sense, I think that childhood obesity might be the cause of high blood pressure, not some new genetic flaw recently uncovered by our friends in the pharmaceutical industry.

I would expect in the next three to six months a drug company to release a drug to combat this growing problem. Conspiracy yes, but I find it a little weird that the majority of the sponsors for the nightly news were pharmaceutical companies and a major story was featuring a societal problem that drugs should not be the solution.

If your kid has high blood pressure, change their diet. Reduce their intake of carbohydrates and sugar and move them to a more fat, protein, reduced carbohydrate diet.

I no longer watch the evening news. I'm not a fake news radical, but I do believe there are other news sources on other platforms that provide a more accurate and unbiased version of our world.

The next time you watch the evening news, if you are a part of my demographic that still has this habit, watch the number of drug ads and then see if maybe, just maybe, there is a story on a "new epidemic" coming to our amazing country.

When that epidemic hits, the drug companies will be waiting to offer your child a $110.87 a month medicine to help cure their growing problem.

As a parent, you are supposed to do everything you can to help and support your kids, and if you know there is a drug to help them, by all means, you better buy it.

Another option might be to get junior or sissy out of the house, to walk, to play, to run, to jump, or to drive past McDonald's to a healthier food choice.

Sorry to offend, just pointing out something that seems a little suspect. Learn proper nutrition, treat your body with respect and love and pass those teachings on to your children.

We have three kids, all in great shape, sans medicine for any ailment.

Teach your children well.

"My mom's a doctor, but because she came from India and then Africa, where childhood obesity was not a problem, she put no premium on having skinny kids. In fact, she and my dad didn't mind having a chubby daughter. Part of me wonders if it even made them feel a little prosperous, like *Have you seen our overweight Indian child? Do you know how statistically rare this is?*"
— **Mindy Kaling**

Amazon Changed Everything

"Never close your lips to those whom you have already opened your heart."

— **Charles Dickens**

We were sitting on our front porch in Indianapolis last night. Winding down our day, chatting about things we needed to do.

I was strumming my guitar and my Queen said: "Our Colorado flag is getting a little worn." I put down my guitar, picked up my phone, went to Amazon and ordered a new $24.99 State of Colorado Flag. It will be delivered today.

We fly a Colorado Flag at our Indy home and an Indiana Flag at our Colorado home.

My Queen was making a list on her paper plate. All our to-do lists are done on paper plates. We started this "ritual" one morning when walking. The paper plate is the ultimate tool to take notes when walking.

If you visit our home, you will see a couple of paper plates with various notes, lists, phone numbers, etc.

I looked at our list and noticed window cleaning. We have a lot of windows; these windows need to be cleaned. So, I went to Google Maps, I typed in Window Cleaning and looked for a location close to us to call.

It was about 7:30 pm and as I was scrolling through the list, I noticed something very troubling. Every window washing company was "CLOSED."

Closed? We live in a 24 / 7 society, a business can never be closed. If I want to schedule my windows to be cleaned, I'd like to get that taken care of at 7:30 on a Tuesday night. I don't want to wait until 9:00 am the next morning.

If you own a company, you no longer have business hours. You are open 24 / 7 and if you are not, your competition will be ready and able to take care of your clients when you "close" your business.

I think our listed office hours are 8:00 to 5:00, I'm going to have one of our interns go deep on the web and eliminate our office hours. We are open 24 / 7. If you need us on a Tuesday night at 8:00 pm, we will welcome your call.

Today, our businesses need to always be open. Not necessarily to allow people to walk in, but if someone is thinking about buying a car, it would be nice to call a car dealership and talk to someone about a car. Think about that new salesman you just hired, flip the phones to his or her cell phone when "closed" and make the available to anyone that wants to chat about their next purchase.

I was heading back from my son's graduation on Saturday. It was about 3:00 pm and I got a call from a client. She had received a notice and had a question, she called our office to leave a message and I answered the phone.

She was shocked. "Sir, I was going to leave a message, I can't believe you answered the phone." I gave her a little guidance, she was very appreciative and said, "I'm calling on behalf of my Mom, but I don't think our insurance carrier would ever answer the phone on a Saturday. I should talk to you guys about our insurance needs."

If you own a business figure out how to NEVER BE CLOSED! Create a policy or procedure that allows for your phones to roll to a responsible party that can help your clients or prospects after hours.

Your business is never closed. You are always open to help people that need your knowledge and skill set.

If you are a financial planner, you might want to be open 24 / 7.

If you are an accountant, you might want to be open 24 / 7.

If you are a tech company, you might want to be open 24 / 7.

If you sell plumbing supplies, you might want to be open 24 / 7.

If you serve the trash hauling industry, you might want to be open 24 / 7.

If you operate a nonprofit, you might want to be open 24 / 7.

Banks, law offices, consultants, electrical contractors, construction firms, if you are in business I plead with you to open your office online and via phone 24 / 7.

If someone needs your services, we no longer have the luxury of being closed. Closing our businesses is no longer an option.

If you want to thrive in today's business environment, never close your lips to those whom you have already opened your heart."

Is it time you hired your first coach?

"If you have a dream, don't just sit there. Gather courage to believe that you can succeed and leave no stone unturned to make it a reality."
— **Roopleen**

I had a coaching meeting yesterday. I worked with my coach on planning the next five years of my life. We talked about my aspirations, company goals, and what we need to do to hit those marks.

Today, I have three coaches. I'm not ashamed; I need help, these three individuals' help has helped me dramatically, so why not use a third party to make yourself or your company better?

I was sitting at Eureka restaurant on the 4th of July. It's a little place in Boulder, Colorado on Pearl Street. It's one of our spots. We were sitting at the bar eating lunch, and there was a documentary on about Andre Agassi. They were interviewing Andre and his wife Steffi Graf, but they also interviewed his coaches.

As I sat there, I realized that top performers need coaches. Top performers can't be who they are without coaches.

Every top professional athlete has a coach or two to help them see things they cannot see.

When was the last time you let someone into your life to help you? To help you see the things you cannot see. We, humans, have blinders and sometimes it takes an unbiased 3rd party to listen, watch, and point out things you may be missing.

I have a coach for our company. That coach helps Jen and I make sure we have the best plan, and we also execute on that plan.

I have a personal coach that challenges me to become a better human being.

And I have a sales coach helping me with my team of sales people making sure our newer sales people are on track to hit their goals.

I would like to claim full credit for the last few year's successes, but for me, it's about my team of advisors, my YODA's, that have helped me and my company reach that next level.

I would be remiss if I didn't point out I have the most amazing partner, but even she has blinders that need to be challenged. My coaches work with us helping us see the things we cannot see.

Coaching is a big thing in Colorado. All my coaches are in the Denver area. But, my first coach was in Indianapolis. I've used a coach for the past 20 years and would not have achieved 25% of my personal or professional goals sans a coach.

No matter who you are, you could improve your life position hiring a coach.

Where in your life do you need help?

Maybe you need help with your relationship with your significant other.

Maybe you need help working on your lumpy meat sack.

Maybe you need help with your business or to have better time management.

No matter the issue, there is a coach that can help you get on track.

Your coach need not be local, most of my coaching is done over the phone or using virtual meetings.

So, what's the cost of a coach? Well, most coach's fees are between $100.00 and $250.00 an hour. But you only use these folks once or twice a month.

Investing $200.00 or $500.00 in yourself or company can prove to be a priceless investment.

Don't be ashamed to ask for help. We all need it. We all have areas that we need help, and as soon as you can admit I need help, the sooner the help can be applied to make your life better.

If you are looking for a coach, I know several. I know a coach that uses hand analysis to help you follow your true-life path. I know this sounds like hippy-dippy-bull-shit, but I know Jayne, have experienced her impact on others; her methods work and have helped others in an amazingly positive way.

If you are looking for a coach to help you with your personal or professional sales, I have those folks as well.

If you are looking for a coach to help you or your company with your financial matters, I have a few coach friends that can jump in and simply help you figure out your income statement, balance sheet, and cash flow statement.

We all need help; we cannot be the best we can be without the help of others. These words are meant to inspire you to begin thinking about what kind of coach you need today. Once you hire your first coach, you might, like me, hire a second and maybe a third.

Don't be ashamed; message me if you need a coach and I'll connect you with the one or two I think can help you. This morning, I'm here to help my dear readers see things they cannot see on their own. This morning this message is for you.

"If you have a dream, don't just sit there. Gather courage to believe that you can succeed and leave no stone unturned to make it a reality."
— **<u>Roopleen</u>**

Complete Failures, a Filthy Secret, and Hypocrisy

"Success is not final, failure is not fatal: it is the courage to continue that counts."
— **Winston S. Churchill**

I'm flying at 30,000 feet, I'm going to share a message with you that might just change your life.

As I was logging into the United Airways Wi-Fi, I was not successful. So, I tried again and again, failed.

I tried a third time and had some success. Try, try, and try again until you succeed.

I'm getting old, my eyes are getting worse, I think that might have had something to do with my repeated failure. But I didn't give up. I never give up.

You are going to fail, failure is part of success. No one has ever succeeded without some failure.

As you go about your day, embrace your failures. Failures are lessons, little classes that are FREE to help you learn what not to do in the future.

There are many stories of people that failed multiple times before achieving success. Successful people are complete failures. They have failed so many times, they have completely failed and once you have completely failed, you learn the ultimate lesson and you succeed.

If you are not successful, you just have not failed enough.

We all have a different view of success. To me, success is having the freedom to do what you want, when you want, every day. That's freedom and to me, freedom is success.

I don't work, I live. I'm a father, lover, writer, speaker, and small business owner. I'm going to spend the next 4 days in Fort Lauderdale, Florida. My partner and I are heading to see one of our 3 kids.

I've got a few opportunities to bring on a few new clients next week. My team is working diligently to put us in a position of success.

We might fail, but as I stated before, those are simply lessons. When we lose, we win a lesson.

I just got a call from an employee, she made a mistake. She under quoted an account by $300.00. My reply was, "you are human, you are going to make mistakes, and it's not a big deal." I gave her a rather simple solution and we will figure out how to fix her error, but she learned a lesson.

Well, she learned two lessons, measure twice and when she makes a mistake she will get grace from her owners. I make mistakes every day. I am not in a position to criticize others for doing the same thing I do. I think that's called hypocrisy.

There seems to be a lot of hypocrisy today, people talking out of both sides of their mouths. I think we are living in a failed time, but this failed time will eventually lead to success.

So, never quit. Never give up. When you think you are done, do it again, and again and learn from your experience. Life is a continuous series of lessons.

Sometimes you win and sometimes you lose, but the people that never quit, those previously complete failures are amazingly successful people.

Oh, and about that filthy secret...

I view myself as a complete failure. I'm going to keep trying, and one day, just maybe...

"Success is not final, failure is not fatal: it is the courage to continue that counts."
— Winston S. Churchill

the people that never quit, those previously complete failures are amazingly successful people.

Oh, and about that filthy secret...

I view myself as a complete failure. I'm going to keep trying, and one day, just maybe...

"Success is not final, failure is not fatal: it is the courage to continue that counts."
— **Winston S. Churchill**

Guns and Roses, The Cult of Ignorance, How to Build a GREAT Team

"There is a cult of ignorance in the United States, and there has always been. The strain of anti-intellectualism has been a constant thread winding its way through our political and cultural life, nurtured by the false notion that democracy means that 'my ignorance is just as good as your knowledge."
— **Isaac Asimov**

5:09 am, coconut oil infused coffee in hand. I got in a little late last night; I went to see Guns and Roses. Great show; catch it if you can.

I've learned in life if you want to play, you better be able to get up the next morning and so here I sit.

We were having one of our meetings yesterday when one of our team members said, "I'm glad I work out, eat right, and get enough sleep. If I didn't, I don't think I could keep up this pace."

I added, "if you are not in pretty good shape, you can't keep up our pace."

Our day typically starts at 5:00 am, we work from our condo until 8:00 and then head out to appointments. Yesterday, we ran five appointments; today is very similar.

We talk to, in many cases, strangers. Strangers that need or want our services. Our job is to talk to strangers and make sure our clients are getting the attention from our team.

I'd never really thought about our pace until K.C. brought it up. He calls it running and gunning. He, like us, is an early riser. When you build your team, find people that share your pace.

K.C. has spent the last two years sitting in a cubical, managing accounts, talking to people on the phone, helping clients with their service needs.

But when we bought the agency from our friend, we needed to have an employee that was familiar with the clients; we needed a team member that could help transition our new clients into our system.

But a funny thing happened with K.C.; we learned he had a pretty amazing sales skill set. I learned he was an entrepreneur and had the makings of a great sales person.

How did we figure this little "secret out"? Well, we ran a DISC profile. His results came back High D and High I. That mirrors my Queen and my DISC profile. Our team in Colorado consists of 3 people that are all get it done, early risers, "let's build something special" mentality.

We have another new Colorado team member; she's a high I. If you are confused by my D's, and my I's, research DISC profiles, it's a tool you can use to make sure you have the right people in the right seats on the bus.

Her job is to find our Colorado and our Midwest producers strangers. She calls strangers, finds pain, and then sets an appointment for us to see if people need our help.

Many times, a company is not running at capacity because they have the wrong people in the wrong seats on the bus. You might have an amazing team, but if you have your quarterback playing wide receiver, and your running back punting your ball, you have some issues.

There are 7 billion people in this world, and it's a cop out to say there are no good people to help you run or grow your company. There are great people all around, but it is up to you to find them.

Quit bitching, moaning, and complaining that you can't find good people. Instead, begin looking for great people. They exist, they are usually working for someone else, but they might be in the wrong seat on another company's bus.

An owner of a business is nothing more than a talent coordinator. One of your jobs as an owner of a company is to seek out great people to help grow your team.

If you have a team member that's heart is no longer aligned with your goals, help them find a new vocation and back fill that position with someone that has passion.

We've upgraded our team this year with five new fresh faces. Faces that are aligned with our goals, faces that are excited to run, gun, and help us find the pain, heal the pain, and show the love.

Building a team starts with building a great culture. Build a culture that allows for the personal and professional growth of your team. What is your company culture? Why in the world would anyone want to join your company?

Culture is king, but so is getting the right people in the right seats on your bus. You can figure this out using Meyers Briggs and DISC profiles.

Test your current team, have an outside third party review the results and then hold an hour or two-hour meeting to help everyone remember how to communicate with each other.

We are all different, but we are also very similar. If you can figure out how to connect and communicate with your team and allow your team to understand better how to connect with each other, it's one of the first steps to building a great team.

Our company will be featured on the cover of a national magazine next month. The article has been written, the photo shoot was fun, and next month our industry will learn a little more about those "hippies" that run their company different than most.

Create a company culture that will have great people calling you to join your company. Create a plan that helps identify where those great people fit into your culture.

We did, we do, and for us, it has made all the difference.

"There is a cult of ignorance in the United States, and there has always been. The strain of anti-intellectualism has been a constant thread winding its way through our political and cultural life, nurtured by the false notion that democracy means that 'my ignorance is just as good as your knowledge."
— **Isaac Asimov**

Start with Culture, Kill with Communication

"And a new philosophy emerged called quantum physics, which suggest that the individual's function is to inform and be informed. You really exist only when you're in a field sharing and exchanging information. You create the realities you inhabit."
— **Timothy Leary**

Yesterday was a great day.

We flew some employees in from our Western location. We gathered everyone together and had a company meeting. Our meeting started with this 2-minute video.

https://www.youtube.com/watch?v=tp4mION S51E&t=16s

We used this as an example of our company moving forward. This approach to teamwork is our past present and future.

We talked about where we are and where we are going. We talked about expectations and introduced some of our new team members.

We answered questions about some new policies and procedures we have implemented to make our company more efficient.

After that meeting, we met with our sales team one on one. We reviewed their production, their trajectory, and rewarded some with a growth bonus.

During one of our sales reviews, a team member, one of our rock stars, shared his daily inspiration.

It was a list of things that he reads when he's down. The list was on tattered paper. The words were written down years ago, but have been read many times.

I snapped a photo of the tattered paper to share with one of our team members, "things to remember, questions to ask." They are as follows:

- How old would you be if you didn't know your age?
- What would you do differently if you knew no one would judge you?
- Are you holding on to something you should let go of?
- What do you love and what are you doing about it?
- Do you ask engaging questions? Do you settle for what you know?
- When was the last time you tried something new?
- Are you aware that someone has it worse than you?
- Do you celebrate all the things you do have?

We are staffed with the best staff in the insurance industry. We are picky about our staff and only allow people in that fit our culture. Culture is king.

If you own a company, do your employees know where you are and where you are going?

Do you communicate the positives and negatives of your marketplace and the opportunities that are present?

Do you ask your employees what motivates them? Do they give you tattered pieces of paper that help show what drives them?

As business owners, we have an opportunity to lead. We can lead our teams, communicate our dreams, and allow them to be a part of an amazing future.

It starts with culture and ends with communication.

If you have culture and communicate within that culture, nothing can stop your company from amazing success.

Get busy fellow business owners, there is gold at the end of the rainbow. Enjoy your journey and allow your team to enjoy the journey as well.

Lead with clear communication, create a culture that fosters personal and professional growth and then... get the hell out of the way.

"And a new philosophy emerged called quantum physics, which suggest that the individual's function is to inform and be informed. You really exist only when you're in a field sharing and exchanging information. You create the realities you inhabit."
— **Timothy Leary**

Culture and Building a Team

"Well, for one thing, the culture we have does not make people feel good about themselves. We're teaching the wrong things. And you have to be strong enough to say if the culture doesn't work, don't buy it. Create your own. Most people can't do it."
— **Mitch Albom**

We added a couple new team members yesterday. That's a total of 4 new people in the last 60 days.

The one thing I hear from other business owners is "finding talented people that fit one's culture is hard."

I agree it's a struggle to find new folks, but I think we might have found a couple rock stars.

One is a young man, 21 years of age. An actuary student at Ball State University. He was looking for an internship and after meeting him, we crafted a 12-week program that will allow him to touch and taste every aspect of our company.

He was referred by his uncle, a friend of mine. His aunt just so happens to work in our company. He comes from a great family. He's smart, eager to learn, and will be a great addition to our team.

The other new addition is a female looking for a home. She has run her own business for a few years, she's had great success, but she's been on an island, fighting the good fight alone.

We talked about her skill set, how it might mesh with our team, and crafted a plan to have her meet our team and get acclimated to our culture.

She will soon meet with the rest of our staff, forming a relationship with each teammate, learning their passion, their strengths, and weaknesses.

It's time to grow your team.

It's time to look outside and find someone or a few someone's to help you grow your vision.

I met with a new business owner last week. He too is building his team. He's starting from scratch. He had a small base but just added financial and operations.

In every successful company, you usually have a core competency of finance, sales, and operations.

Once you fill these seats, you can move on and look for excellent customer service and finally quality control.

That's it; if you fill your company with those five skill sets you will achieve success.

I'm off to Baltimore. I'm taking my partner to see Jackson Browne for her birthday.

Take it easy.

"Well, for one thing, the culture we have does not make people feel good about themselves. We're teaching the wrong things. And you have to be strong enough to say if the culture doesn't work, don't buy it. Create your own. Most people can't do it."
— **Mitch Albom**

Listen with Your Eyes — Have the Courage to be Curious

"For what it's worth: it's never too late or, in my case, too early to be whoever you want to be. There's no time limit, stop whenever you want. You can change or stay the same, there are no rules to this thing. We can make the best or the worst of it. I hope you make the best of it. And I hope you see things that startle you. I hope you feel things you never felt before. I hope you meet people with a different point of view. I hope you live a life you're proud of. If you find that you're not, I hope you have the courage to start all over again."
— **Eric Roth**

We were out to dinner with some new friends last night. We were talking about some recent experiences at an Escape Room.

My partner and one of the other folks had been to an Escape Room in Indianapolis, they were sharing their experience.

According to both our experienced Escape Room veterans, we should all try the experience, both said it was "awesome!"

If you are not familiar with the Escape Room concept, it's a business that usually has 3 or 4 rooms each set with a theme. Most communities now have an Escape Room. My friend Kathie opened one in Muncie, Indiana.

Each room has clues and your team has to figure out the clues to "escape" from the room. If you get stuck, you can ask for help and someone in the control room can give you a little hint.

Our friend, Rick, described his experience to us. His team had a leader and the leader was directing everyone. As the leader was commanding the team, Rick walked through the room checking things out.

Rick said, "I'm curious by nature, I like to push buttons, flip levers, and investigate my surroundings."

As the leader was leading, Rick was walking around the room just being his normal curious self.

As the team was working on solving the first riddle, Rick pushed a button. The button opened a secret door to another room. The other room was not the escape but held many clues as to how to escape from the main room.

The team escaped in record time, not because of leadership, but because a rogue team member got curious.

Curiosity killed the cat, but it rarely kills humans and when it does, it's usually an epic death. We are all going to die, so if you are killed being curious, it might be a rather fun way to go.

I don't think most people are curious anymore. We live our life within our lanes, making sure we don't get "out of line," but we miss so damn much that life has to offer.

Today, I'm asking you to live curiously. Look for buttons to push, look for that hidden lever to pull, that item that looks out of place.

Through curiosity, we can learn about our world, but we can also learn about ourselves.

Every day you drive the same way to work. Today, go a different route. Take the road less traveled, be like Bobby Frost and go that different path and you might be surprised at what you find.

Listen to people. When they say something you don't understand, don't just nod your head and go on, ask them to clarify.

If someone tells you something, they are telling you that for a reason. There is something bigger than all of us, there is some sort of collective thinking going on between us humans and if you hear a nugget of information that sounds odd, out of place, or you wonder why they shared that nugget of info, probe. Go deeper, listen with your eyes, what does their body language tell you?

If you own a company, send one of your employees out on a mission. Ask them to simply be curious. Ask them to take a couple hours, and for the benefit of the company go out, seek knowledge and return with their findings and share with your team.

A few thousand years ago, this was how tribes gained territory. There were no Google maps, there were no photos of the jungle next door, there were no books describing what we might find by seeking. It was incumbent on the humans to be curious to explore their world. It was incumbent on the humans to be curious to expand their world.

When was the last time you were curious? When was the last time you found that secret lever or button and pushed it?

If you are like most people, it's been a few years. We are most curious when we are children, but as we age we get more confident with our knowledge of our world. We stop seeking answers and let things simply be.

Stop letting it be. Listen with your eyes today. Go to a different Starbucks, try a new drink, or eat at a different restaurant for lunch, the world is a big place and our acceptance of how things work limits our understanding of our world.

No matter who you are and no matter how old you are, living curious can expand your world. It can open your mind to new realities and opportunities that you would miss by simply listening to leadership.

It's time to reconnect with that curious nature you had as a small child. You are missing so damn much of life not looking around, not asking questions, and not pushing that button that seems out of place.

Well, that's it. That's the message for this beautiful amazing morning. I hope this message resonates with you, I hope you find joy in being a little more curious and I hope that your curiosity does not kill you, but makes you stronger.

"For what it's worth: it's never too late or, in my case, too early to be whoever you want to be. There's no time limit, stop whenever you want. You can change or stay the same, there are no rules to this thing. We can make the best or the worst of it. I hope you make the best of it. And I hope you see things that startle you. I hope you feel things you never felt before. I hope you meet people with a different point of view. I hope you live a life you're proud of. If you find that you're not, I hope you have the courage to start all over again."
— **Eric Roth**

Live Curious

"I have no special talents. I am only passionately curious."
— Albert Einstein

I met with one of our new salesmen this week. It's time for them to leave the nest. He has been training for 8 months, learning the intricate parts of our business; what is good, what is bad, how to approach certain types of accounts. I gave him a little advice, not much. I told him to be curious.

He will create his own way. My job is to watch, observe, and tweak his style to allow him the greatest success. I think I have a Michael Jordan of sales on my hands, but time will tell.

Sales are nothing more than curiosity. Well, curiosity with a conversation. Imagine yourself as a child and your neighbor just got a new car.

You would be curious. You would walk over and start asking questions. You would show an interest; your neighbor would be proud to tell you about their new toy.

You would want to know where it came from, how fast it goes, can you hear it run? You would have an interest in your neighbor, they would appreciate the interest and they would be kind and tell you about their new purchase.

That's sales.

When you are a small child, your parents tell you not to talk to strangers, but when you enter the sales world, you are told: "go talk to stranger.".

It's funny to me the value salespeople put on prospecting. Very few of the sales people I know actually prospect. They wait for the call to come in, the referral from a friend, but that is not sales. That is being lazy.

Professional sales are being curious enough to ask a question.

The most successful sales people I know continuously prospect. They are constantly seeking new opportunities for people they do not know.

Let's be careful and realize that sales are not about selling people stuff. People hate to be sold, but they love to buy. If you want to sell things, you will come across as a salesperson.

If you approach the world as if you are looking for people to converse with and see if there is anything you can do to help them, that is professional sales.

I teach a pretty rigid prospecting approach that if followed, will provide unlimited income to the person that applies the "system."

Prospecting is nothing more than talking to strangers. If you approach every prospect with the goal of having a conversation, there is no pressure. You are only trying to engage someone.

I was in a steam room yesterday at my local YMCA. There was a man in there, I had seen him before, but I did not know him. I asked him "What's your name?" He replied "Steve." We went on to chat about who we were, what we did, how long we had been coming to the YMCA.

I was curious as to who this man was. It took 3 words to start a conversation. I'll see Steve around, I'll call him by name. I don't wish to sell Steve anything, I don't know what he needs. But that type of activity open doors into other lives.

How many times in a given day are you in a position to be curious? You are surrounded by people, places, and things (aka nouns) that you may or may not know. If you know them, be kind, talk to them. If you don't, learn about them. Ask questions, introduce yourself.

Welcome to the world of curious prospecting.

"I have no special talents. I am only passionately curious."
— Albert Einstein

That Damn 1%.

"You may say I'm a dreamer, but I'm not the only one. I hope someday you'll join us. And the world will live as one."
— **John Lennon**

Sitting in Florida, visiting a kid; the final volleyball season of her life starts today. We thought we would head down for the day and catch a game.

We flew in yesterday morning, worked, then took our daughter out for some Italian food.

As I was sitting in the restaurant, I looked around and noticed the diversity surrounding me.

There were white people, and there were black people. There were Cubans, and some people that I could not detect their tribe, but they were something.

We all sat in the same location; we dined, we all laughed, there were no punches thrown, we all enjoyed our food and beverages.

You would think in our society today, that scene is impossible. The thought of many people of various colors and ideas sharing a space without violence is almost a dream.

If you watch the news, we should have been punching each other, screaming, and fighting about pronouns or ideology.

But we didn't, we just ate sans free of violence.

Look, we are all different. Men are different from women. A person born in Indiana is different than a person born in Boston. An inner city young black child has a far different frame of reference than one brought up in a private school in Southern California.

Instead of focusing on our differences, why not celebrate our unique life experiences.

Let's agree to approach each other with kindness and an open mind to the other person's views and ideas.

Not all ideas are created equal if you are educated and can explain your views, you have the ability to change other's minds. Listen, open your mind to another view and maybe, just maybe you will think differently than you did before the conversation.

The world is not what the media would have you believe. The narrative of two worlds is getting a little overblown.

When was the last time you witnessed violence or rage? If you turn off the television, your computer, or phone, you will see people living peacefully, talking, eating, and laughing.

It struck me last night how damn peaceful and amazing our world is, and it's time someone pointed out that our world is not as "jacked up" as some make it seem.

People dining in a restaurant peacefully is not a good story. It won't get clicks, there is no reason to share my story, but that is the story. That is life.

There were no signs; there was no one getting shot in the crotch with a rubber bullet, there was simply people with different ideas and genetic makeup collectively doing what we humans do.

The next time you see a story about violence and rage, stop and look around. Is that your life or is that the life that others want you to believe?

Our world is amazing. Our world is peaceful; our world is a collection of different people with different ideas and 99% of the time those ideas are shared without violence.

It's that damn 1% that we tend to focus on, and it's got to stop. It's always that 1%. Let's start focusing on the 99% and understand our world is awesome.

Yes, there are differences, but there are many similarities. Stop trying to war with your neighbor for who they voted for, what they believe, or the God they worship.

Celebrate diversity, learn from your neighbor. Enjoy the peace that 99% of the world experiences on a daily basis and let those that love strife live their sad, pitiful lives.

Be kind. Enjoy your fellow humans. We did, we do, and for us, that has made all the difference.

"You may say I'm a dreamer, but I'm not the only one. I hope someday you'll join us. And the world will live as one."
— **John Lennon**

That Damn Insurance Company

"Let us toast to animal pleasures, to escapism, to rain on the roof and instant coffee, to unemployment insurance and library cards, to absinthe and good-hearted landlords, to music and warm bodies and contraceptives... and to the "good life," whatever it is and wherever it happens to be."
— **Hunter S. Thompson**

I have a good friend and client. He is from Guatemala but has been a U.S. Citizen for 20 years.

About three years ago, a young man stopped by his house and told him he had roof damage. We submitted a claim to his insurance carrier, and the claim was denied. There was no damage; the report showed as much, his roof was 20 plus years old, he needed a new roof.

Two years ago, another young man stopped by and shared the same story. My friend, now thinking he had new damage called me, we turned in the claim, and the claim was denied again.

Last Saturday a 3rd young man stopped by my friend's house, advised he had damage and submitted a claim to his insurance company.

An independent firm, ironically owned by another friend, did the inspection, took the photos and again reported to the carrier there was no storm damage, it was simply a 25-year-old roof that needed to be replaced.

After three submitted claims, and knowing our client's roof was 25 years old, the company sent a nonrenewal notice.

At this point, I'll stop and say this is why many people hate the insurance industry. We never pay claims, but sometimes, we should not pay claims.

The carrier in question is a carrier that goes over and above trying to pay claims. If there is a way, they pay.

On this last claim, the young man got the carrier information and submitted the claim on a Saturday morning.

We received the nonrenewal and 3rd loss notice the same day. My friend called me a little upset. I phoned the "storm chaser" the most recent young man that was intent on selling a roof and taking advantage of my friend and client.

He was a nice young man, explained that if our company adjuster didn't agree, they had contracts with "public adjusters" that would agree with their assessment.

I called the carrier and reviewed the claim file. The report shows no storm damage, just an old roof that needed to be replaced.

I called my client on Thursday and spoke openly and honestly about our situation. I said "there are people in this world that try and take advantage of others. I think this is one of those times."

My client said, "I've thought that might be the case." His neighbor just got a new roof, he already had the business card of the roofing company, and he called them and is getting an estimate to the replace his roof.

I'm going to get the nonrenewal rescinded based on his "new risk management approach" and get him back with his correct risk management provider.

The insurance industry gets a bad rap, but in many cases, it's people trying to take advantage of others preying on their lack of understanding of what or what is not a true claim.

I'm writing in defense of all my fellow insurance providers to shine a light on "storm chasers" and others who are perpetrating or attempting to perpetrate insurance fraud.

When you believe you have a claim, work with your insurance agent. After 21 years in this business, I'm no longer going to accept "you have roof damage" claims.

We are changing our internal policy to help avoid this type of situation in the future. If you have damage, we will now have a second opinion "qualified contractor" view any and all damage to qualify we have damage, and we are not dealing with a wear and tear issue.

Insurance does not pay for everything, if it did, it would not be affordable. I've been in this industry for more than half my life, and in the majority of the cases, I've seen our carriers pay the claims that needed to be paid.

Insurance is there when you need it. It's expensive, but I promise my clients and the clients of my fellow insurance providers, if you have a legitimate claim, it will be paid.

"Let us toast to animal pleasures, to escapism, to rain on the roof and instant coffee, to unemployment insurance and library cards, to absinthe and good-hearted landlords, to music and warm bodies and contraceptives... and to the "good life," whatever it is and wherever it happens to be."
— **Hunter S. Thompson**

Dare to Dare! Beyond Discipline and Creativity

"I believe that the most important single thing, beyond discipline and creativity, is daring to dare."
— **Maya Angelou**

I have a new friend. Well, actually a team member and a friend. He's smart, accomplished, and motivated.

The universe has a way of putting people in our lives that can help us learn. I think with our new team member, he came to us to learn, but also to teach.

We have been spending a lot of time together. We bought an agency, he was managing the clients prior to our purchase. He knows the people, he has the relationship, and he's introducing me to our new clients.

We've spent a few hours in the car the last few days and it's refreshing to hear his take and views on life.

He was raised in Denver, attended school by our new office, left to get an education in southern Texas and then played professional basketball overseas in France. He has a beautiful life experience.

As we were talking yesterday, we were discussing all the distractions men have on a daily basis. No matter your age, nature is always at work.

My new friend said, "it's all about discipline." We talked a lot about discipline. What it means. The importance of having values and sticking to those values.

If your life is not what you want it to be, I would ask how disciplined are you? Can you make a decision and stick with that decision?

As humans, we are tempted to do things that might not be in our best interests. Eating that doughnut for breakfast, skipping that workout, taking our time and arriving late for an appointment.

We all have choices and the more disciplined we are with our thoughts, ideas, and actions, the more success we can welcome into our lives.

I think another thing that is equally important in life is being creative. You have a mind, use it. We are in the process of eliminating all paper in our company. I know, it's way past time, but soon, we will not have to mess with those by-products of trees.

We are going to get creative with technology and remove 90% of all paper from our company. I'm the reason we still use dead trees. But working in two states has caused yours truly to determine we have to change our process.

We have to be disciplined and we have to be creative when implementing our new process.

When was the last time you created something? I mean truly created something from thin air? I'm doing it right now. I'm pulling words from the air, organizing them into some barely readable content that a few people will enjoy.

I create daily. This creation sparks me to think differently the rest of my day. I open my mind at 5:00 am and mind dump those thoughts or ideas that I can't seem to let go.

It takes discipline to write every day, but between you and me, it's easy for me. Maybe you are not a writer, but you are a creator. You can create, but what is it that your God, the Universe, or that Purple Monkey Driving Your Life Bus gave you as your creation skill?

We all have it. We all can create and we all have the discipline to execute our creativity.

My life moving forward will be that of a personal developer of people. I'm changing my role of strictly selling and moving towards the development of our people and our company.

I love sales, but it's time for me to move forward and begin shaping our next team of owners, managers, and sale people.

It will take discipline and I'll have to be creative with each and every human I work with. Humans are unique and need different teaching tools to reach their goals.

I dare you to instill greater discipline in your life.
I dare you to create.

Only after you embrace these two little ideas can you begin to dare to dare.

"I believe that the most important single thing, beyond discipline and creativity, is daring to dare."
— **Maya Angelou**

Dead Fish and 2 years, 7 months, and 3 Days Until Retirement

"Confront the dark parts of yourself, and work to banish them with illumination and forgiveness. Your willingness to wrestle with your demons will cause your angels to sing."
— **August Wilson**

Yesterday, I met a man that is two years, seven months, and three days away from his retirement.

He was my UBER driver. He was also a firefighter. I listened as he described his plans to move south in 2 years, seven months, and three days.

I listened and smiled and even said: "it sounds like you have everything figured out." He replied, "yes, but it only takes one thing to blow everything up."

He dropped me off at my appointment, and I felt a little sad for my new friend. He's miserable in his job, so much he has counted down the days until he can get his "gold watch."

I've written before; I love my work. I love my vocation, my job, my opportunity to help others manage their risk.

I do not have a clock running on when I will stop my "work." I plan on working, in some capacity, until I die.

To me, work gives us value. Work is not something that should be loathed but enjoyed like one's relationship with their significant other.

If you don't love your work, please for the sake of humanity, quit and find a job or opportunity that brings you joy.

I don't understand why you would spend the majority of your time doing something you do not enjoy.

I was listening to a podcast the other day. They were talking about trust fund kids and how many fail to have a positive life experience.

These are kids that from the time of their birth, they are given a stream of income to do whatever, wherever, however, they choose. They can do anything but most end up with drug or alcohol issues.

It turns out that living without work or a purpose does not end well for our fellow humans.

I had a client a few years ago. He had a successful business. He ran it until he was about 65 and then shut it down to retire. About a month or so after he retired, he had a heart attack and died.

I'm sure there was no direct correlation between his death and his retirement, but I often wondered if

"Bob" had no retired if he would still be around running his company, helping his local community.

Work gives meaning and purpose to an otherwise meaningless and purposeless life. If you do not enjoy your work, find a job or do a job that brings you joy and happiness.

You have a unique skill set. How can you use those skills to better humanity? What kind of job or duty could you do on a daily basis that would allow you happiness and impact the lives of others?

Forget about money. Once you work with passion, money will follow. If you have less money, simply adjust your lifestyle to match the lower number of dollars in your bank account.

Happiness trumps wealth. Most wealthy people are not as happy as those with less money. Time ran a story that claimed, "Suicides are more common in richer neighborhoods."

http://business.time.com/2012/11/08/why-suicides-are-more-common-in-richer-neighborhoods/

It seems that keeping up with the Joneses is not a meaningful existence. Stop trying to match others and focus on yourself and your gifts to create a life that brings value and purpose.

Here's an idea, only dead fish go with the flow. Don't be a dead fish. Live, have a purpose, do something that gives your happiness.

You do not have to sit in that cubical dealing with all that office drama to be happy or, maybe I should say, miserable.

These words are for you, the tired, the unhappy, and the "I hate my job," the two years, seven months, and three days' people that are simply biding their time.

There is a group of humans that have figured out that life is grander when doing something you love. Stop working at a job or vocation you hate and find something that brings you and those around you joy and happiness.

Live and work with passion.

"Confront the dark parts of yourself, and work to banish them with illumination and forgiveness. Your willingness to wrestle with your demons will cause your angels to sing."
— **August Wilson**

The Death of "The Office"

"Time to leave now, get out of this room, go somewhere, anywhere; sharpen this feeling of happiness and freedom, stretch your limbs, fill your eyes, be awake, wider awake, vividly awake in every sense and every pore."
— **Stefan Zweig**

My monthly peer group met this week. I've written before about my peer group. It's a collection of business owners that meet monthly to review each other's financials, talk through challenges, and provide accountability when needed.

One of our members is selling his firm. The new owners have decided that they are going to relocate to some new office space.

I understand the want for a change. New owners, new location, new direction. I'm sure the new space is cool. I'm sure they will populate the new office with fancy furniture and maybe even add some debt to make sure their new office is "awesome."

But it occurred to me during that discussion that the value of the office has been dramatically reduced in the past few years and I think the days of the "office" are waning.

We just hired a new employee for our Midwest operation. She has experience, she was looking for an opportunity, and she lives about an hour and a half from our Indianapolis location and 3 hours from our Northern Indiana office.

But she has the skills we need, her test results show her to be a good fit for our new position and so we made her an offer and she accepted.

"Ann" won't be working from our office. Ann will be working from home. Some owners might fear this arrangement, but I speak from experience. We've been using telecommuting for about 10 years with various degrees of success.

As we continue to grow in the Midwest and at our Colorado location, our want and need for office space will diminish.

We won't be making major investments in office space anytime soon; most people would prefer to work from home, and if you build systems that allow for the easy flow of information between team members, it removes the need for team proximity.

I'm officially calling today: the start of the death of the office. Why? How can this be?

I'm sure you are a client of UBER but have you ever to UBER's office? If not an UBER client, maybe you have bought something from Amazon. When was the last time you went to Amazon's office?

Remember when you had to go to a bank to actually bank? When was the last time you physically visited a bank?

Our world is changing and the thought of an opulent office, chocked full of fancy ass furniture, large conference rooms, and a great big coffee bar is so 1990's.

It's time to rethink how your firm works and occupies space. Do you need that office space or could you make a small command center where the main mission is to connect your employees through today's technology?

Instead of investing $20K a month in leasing an office, or making a major investment in real estate, why not take that money and invest in a technology platform that would better connect your team? Why not take that money and invest in your people?

As we continue to grow, our team members will be speckled all over the world. No longer are we limited to the people that live in our geographic area to expand our team. If you live in Alaska and have the skill set we need, we would like to talk to you.

I've not met one of my clients at my office for years. Most of my clients don't live or work close to our locations so I visit with them at their office or meet them at a convenient location close to their office.

This idea, this concept might concern you. But the next generation of great team members is not going to want to come to "the office" and sit in a "cube."

The next generation thrives on freedom. They want to be able to move around, get their work done, but on their time and in their environment.

This will not work for every business. My brother-in-law is a dentist. It's rather important that his employees come to his office. A dental assistant working from home would not be optimal for Dr. Ken.

But most businesses, service businesses, banks, accounting, technology, insurance, and a host of other verticals are losing the need for that "office" space.

People are going to start demanding online ordering. Even some wholesalers are moving to a drop ship method of sale never touching the inventory they sell.

In the future, people will demand you bring the product to them. They will demand that you have online systems that make it easy to get your product and services.

I'm not making any bold prediction. This has been forecasted for years, but it's starting to really take hold.

Stop investing in that office space. Start investing in your people and connecting them through technology.

The world is changing, the world is evolving, and in order to keep up, today's business must evolve or go the way of Sears, JC Penny, and Kmart.

These three titans of retail did not see the coming online purchase of items. These three titans will soon be a memory.

Don't let your company be a memory, begin adjusting your services not around a location, but around your people.

"Time to leave now, get out of this room, go somewhere, anywhere; sharpen this feeling of happiness and freedom, stretch your limbs, fill your eyes, be awake, wider awake, vividly awake in every sense and every pore."
— **Stefan Zweig**

The Gift of Death

"Who wants to live forever?"
— **Freddie Mercury**

New year, so let's tackle death. Oh, wait, did you come here for some happy shiny insight for this new year of opportunity? Hold on, give this message some time.

You are going to die. Right now, you are nothing more than a collection of cells loosely placed together on a blue ball hurtling through infinity.

At some point, this loose association of cells will detach and leave only your conscious, soul, or whatever you deem your true self. A lot of people died in 2016 and a lot will die in 2017.

We humans love to die not as if we had an alternative path. But if we did, would we take it?

There is something comforting about knowing this is only for a brief time. That everything you know, feel, taste, and touch will one day be gone. Wait, is that a comfort to you or a horrific idea that once this body dies, it's all over?

I, for one, love the idea of death. It makes me aware that my time on this earth is limited. It is a reminder that every moment of every day I need to do something to leave a positive impact.

Death is actually a gift. If we lived forever, what reason would you have to squeeze life's sponge?

Let me help you if you are in the latter group. If you are scared to die, let me remind you that you actually die twice.

You die when your physical body stops working and you die again the last time your given name is mentioned.

For most, it might last a generation, maybe two, but at some point, no one will know your name; your legacy will be covered with dust, your input and actions that seemed so damn important whilst on this earth will be nothing but myths.

We were talking about death last night and it occurred to me that my children probably do not know their great-grandparent's names. I know these names, I will say these names, but without my passing this information along, my great-grandparents will die the second death with me.

Teach your children well. Tell them about your grandparents, mention their name, allow them to know the names and share with their children. Help those that helped make you live another generation.

New Year's Eve 2016 was a beautiful night. We hung out with some kids, drank Kombucha in Champaign flutes and rang in the New Year.

If you are waking up feeling like crap, next year replace your booze with Kombucha and wake up feeling amazing.

As we were sipping the life juice, we purchased a Quello (www.quello.com) membership and started watching the thousands upon thousands of hours of concert footage of our favorite bands.

As we were flipping around, I landed on a Queen show. Queen, one of my favorite bands, has a song titled "Who Wants to Live Forever." It's a beautiful song sung by a man that knew his time was limited.

As we start this New Year, remember, your time on this spinning blue ball is limited. You only have a short time to leave your mark and some marks will be much larger than others.

Do something that might extend your legacy. Do something this year that might help extend your second death. In 250 years, will your name be mentioned? Will you matter to the future; will your time on this earth impact future generations?

It's New Year's Day. It looks like we are in Colorado with the crisp blue sky, but we are in Indiana. I'd like to think we brought that blue sky to Indiana from Colorado to show our friends what the majority of the days look like at our western home.

The blue crisp sky is a message. It's a reminder to get outside and enjoy the day. It's a little cold, so wear a coat. It's time to move. It's time to evolve. 2017 is a new year and it's time to begin working on your legacy.

I don't think I have ever entered a year with so much optimism. 2016 was my year to set up the next 5 years of my life. I moved 4 times, started a new agency with my partner, published another book, and wrote over 255,000 words of content to feed those that need to be fed.

Yes, 2016 was a magical year, but 2017 holds so much more promise. The promise of multiple new friendships both in Indiana and Colorado. The promise of multiple new business opportunities across the United States.

I'm going to die, so I'm going to do everything I can today and this year to live. Get up off your ass and stop watching TV, that phone, or whatever you've chosen as your device.

Go outside, walk, and work on that lumpy meat sack. Start doing push-ups, planks, and other exercises. Start to meditate and see how quieting your mind for a few minutes each day might impact your day, year, and life.

My friends, this is an amazing time. A time that you get excited to go to the gym for 2 weeks before falling back into old routines. Enjoy the 2 weeks and this year, just maybe, you can make it 3 weeks or maybe the entire first quarter of 2017.

Learn the art of discipline. Do one small thing every day for 30 days and see how your life changes. Get up earlier, go to bed later, change your life on purpose for 30 days straight and see that life is nothing more than a collection of habits.

Habits that you choose to make your life what it is and habits that define who you are as a person.

Be kind. Be joyful. Be present and remember that death is right around the corner. Cheat death by enjoying life and help others live another generation. Speak the names of those you know, but your children do not.

Live, live, live. Come on. I'm going to change the world. Won't you please join me?

"Who wants to live forever?"
— **Freddie Mercury**

M.A.D.? Make a Decision

"Have you ever noticed how 'What the hell' is always the right decision to make?"
— **Terry Johnson (Insignificance)**

There is no wrong decision. No matter what you choose to do, there are no wrong answers, just decisions with consequences.

Successful people make quick decisions.

If you want to improve your life, make quicker decisions.

Where will you eat for lunch? It really doesn't matter.

What will you get your wife for her birthday? It really doesn't matter.

How will you get to work? It really doesn't matter.

Here's an idea, get creative with your decisions. Instead of driving to work, why not UBER? Do you need to drive your car to your office or should you tap into the "new gig society?"

Instead of driving the same path to work this morning, go a different route. Why do you take the same path every day?

You are a creature of habit. You do things over and over again expecting a different result, but that is the definition of insanity.

Make different decisions quicker and your life will change.

I did, I do, and that has made all the difference.

"Have you ever noticed how 'What the hell' is always the right decision to make?"
— **Terry Johnson (Insignificance)**

Confronting Your DEMON

"Confront the dark parts of yourself, and work to banish them with illumination and forgiveness. Your willingness to wrestle with your demons will cause your angels to sing."
— **<u>August Wilson</u>**

We all have demons. I know it's not nice to bring up, but everyone you know has a dark side.

Most of the time we can quell the dark, the bad, the evil, but then it reappears. Not all demons are equal.

There is not a human alive today that does not have some form of anger, fear, or loathing that creeps into your mind and body.

Some of us drink these demons away, others act on these demons, while others suppress the thoughts and ideas until they explode.

We are all good people, I wrote about the 1% the other day. Not the top 1%, by my theory, that 1% of all humans are bad. That's it. 99% of all humans being are good, conscientious, well-meaning people, but even that 99% has a dark side.

Maybe your dark side includes jealous thoughts. Maybe it's envy. Maybe your harbor ill feelings towards a sibling or a parent.

Maybe your dark side includes gluttony. The dark side includes addiction, anger, and hate.

I ask as a writer whose intent is to inspire that you work through your demons. Acknowledge them to an unbiased third party. Your demon or demons are a culmination of your life experiences.

You probably have not gone through life unscathed. Someone or something hurt you and probably hurt you badly, and it's ok. You are not alone; we have all been scarred and bruised at some point in our life.

I think the mistake most people make is that they look at others and think no one else has demons. I'm writing to you this morning to awaken you to the fact, everyone you meet, see, or talk to has demons.

Humans are not perfect; we are flawed, clunky, wonky beings destined to do great things and fail miserably.

Some people seek out faith to help deal with their demons. Religion was created to help quell the demons and give a road map to keep one's life on track.

There are some specific demon management systems. Alcoholics Anonymous is a group that's sole mission is to help people that love their booze manage their addiction.

No matter your demon, there is help available, and it starts with you. Work to understand and be aware of your demons. Acknowledge your imperfections and work to become a better human being.

I'm not judging this morning; I share your plight. I too have my demons, I have done, said, and brought pain and strife into the lives of those I love, and I can't fix my mistakes. I can own my errors and try to learn from my mistakes and become a better man tomorrow.

Don't quit, push through whatever is darkening your life. There is light; I promise you there is light.

It's Monday, August 28, 2017, stop keeping your demons locked in that tiny little box in your head. Open that box, but manage that little bastard. No matter what he or she is, ignorance is bliss, but to improve your life, you have to understand and admit to yourself your failings and continual struggles to be the best human you can be.

People love the angels and hate the demons, but to personally and professionally grow, we have to deal with both.

The dark side exists and the more we can learn and understand our darkness, the better our light will shine.

"Confront the dark parts of yourself, and work to banish them with illumination and

forgiveness. Your willingness to wrestle with your demons will cause your angels to sing."
— **<u>August Wilson</u>**

He didn't show up to the meeting...

"Love truth, but pardon error."
— **Voltaire**

I was to have coffee with a young man yesterday, a leader of a nonprofit in Indianapolis, Indiana.

I was referred to "Alan" by a mutual friend. He thought the two of us should meet for some reason.

I sent an invite, he responded and accepted. We were to meet at Calvin Fletcher's Coffee Company at 1:00 pm.

But yet at 1:00 pm, I sat alone.

I gave it a few moments, sent a text to the number I had. It was a landline so I called.

His assistance said "hold on" and he got on the phone and in agony said, "I'm sorry." He "blew" it, he apologized.

So, now what does one do? I could have gotten upset, but I myself, have "blew or maybe have blown" a meeting a couple times in my life.

We all get busy, we set appointments, we get rocking and at some point, you miss a meeting. It does not happen often, but when it does, you feel terrible. You realize that you screwed up.

I once missed a meeting with Dan Pike, owner of Flow Solutions in Muncie, Indiana and I'm still living it down. Dan's a good friend and we set up the meeting via text, I failed to mark it down and will never forget standing up my friend.

When someone blows a meeting with me, I give grace. I know humans make mistakes. I know that I'm not perfect and expecting perfection of others is an error many people make.

Today, I'll meet that young man; I rescheduled for today. I had a window open, it will actually be a little easier for him in that I'm going to meet him much closer to his office.

Sometime in the next few weeks, someone will blow a meeting with you and I'm asking that you give grace.

Humans make mistakes and although not the norm, it is a part of living in a hectic and chaotic business environment.

I'm sure others might disagree, but for me, giving grace when a fellow human makes the same mistake you have made is an easy decision to make.

So, lighten up. Don't be so damn torched when someone misses a meeting. Give grace.

If they miss two meetings, you may organize the townsfolk and pick up the pitchforks, but for one missed meeting, it's simply a sign of their being a human and not a robot.

"Love truth, but pardon error."
— **Voltaire**

The Discipline of Discipline

"Seek freedom and become captive of your desires. Seek discipline and find your liberty."
— **Frank Herbert**

4:11 am, coconut oil infused coffee cascading down my throat.

It's Monday morning. I did a little work this weekend, but have a few things I needed to tend to this morning.

I usually wake at 5:00, but jumped up an hour early to make sure I was prepared for every meeting today; seems I have a few.

Discipline, it takes discipline to get up at 4:00 am after a long weekend. My partner and I are convinced one of the key traits of a successful person is discipline.

If you commit to doing something, then do it. If you have a job to do, do it; be there on time, maybe a little early, complete the task and move on.

My friends with discipline shine. They succeed. They too wake early, plan their day, and work their plan.

If your life is not what you want it to be, chances are you might be lacking a little discipline.

Maybe you're drinking too much? Take a day, week, or month off and clean out your system. Sobriety takes discipline.

Maybe your body does not look the way you want it to look. Start making small steps towards the body you want. Start walking, then add some exercise, it will take time, but with discipline, you can reshape your body into any configuration you choose.

Maybe your relationship with your mate is not as awesome as it could be. As a man that is still in puppy love after a few years of connecting, true-amazing-crazy-passionate love is a "thing" and I recommend you find it again if somehow it's been lost.

Use some discipline with your work today. Show up a little early and kill that project that has been sitting on your desk the last 3 weeks just waiting to get "wrapped up." Wrap up that project; with discipline one gains the satisfaction of success.

Alright, 4:30 or so, I'm going to wrap this up and get busy. I hope these words resonated, I hope you needed some morning juice.

I did, I do, and writing daily takes discipline. What can you do today to show yourself, maybe remind yourself that you too have strong discipline?

Happy Monday, it's time to roll!

"Seek freedom and become captive of your desires. Seek discipline and find your liberty."
— **Frank Herbert**

Dream or Distraction – The $5654.87 MISTAKE

"No matter where you go or what you do to distract yourself, reality catches up with you eventually."
— **Kody Keplinger**

5:14 am, MCT oil infused coffee in hand and ready for an amazing day.

I had a dream! Just like Martin Luther King, I had a dream. A dream of a day when I would help others create a point of difference.

A dream where I would lead a group of young professionals to reach new heights and impact the lives of young men and women and their future generations.

A dream that would allow me to work with independent insurance agency owners all over the nation. A dream to help them develop their path, not the path followed by most in my industry.

About 9 months ago, I had an idea to create a brand called The Insurance Sherpa. My personal brand is that of an insurance ninja. I know, corny, laughable, not professional, but it works for me.

If I'm a ninja for my clients, I wanted to be a Sherpa for my industry. I had a vision of positioning myself as a thought leader for other insurance agency owners and young agents around the country.

I've been doing "insurance" agency management for 24 years my way and I thought it might be refreshing for others to learn there are multiple paths to success in the insurance industry.

I put together a plan and began to execute. Since I'm a marketing fan I started with a simple logo. I used Up Work to pick a designer. They provided me a few logos, I picked one that I thought represented my new brand and then engaged a friend to help me create my "thought leader" website.

We bought insurancesherpa.net and built a site that included the first four books of my content. I offered my speaking, training, and other services.

Since I write daily, I was going to tweak my daily writings for my fellow insurance agency owners and young agents. Targeting my daily message to that select group of individuals.

I hired a virtual assistant to research what I would need to do to have a weekly podcast.

I had a vision of video sales training for young agents all over the country. I had a vision of setting up a compound in one of my home states, Colorado, and having boot camps for young agents to come and learn from "The Sherpa."

My company, The Thompson Group, has carved a pretty unique position in the insurance world and I wanted to share what we had learned with others.

I didn't think it fair to use The Thompson Group to fund my new brand, so I paid for the project out of my pocket.

As things progressed, I got excited. I even presented my project to one of my peer groups and got some positive reviews of my work.

About the time of "launch," we were finalizing a purchase of a new agency in Colorado. I had to make a choice, spend time on the Sherpa or focus on The Thompson Group and our growth out west. Remember, there are only 24 hours in a day. Sometimes we have to make choices as to the best place to spend our time.

I could have done both, but would not have been great at either. Always remember that good is the enemy of GREAT.

I put Sherpa on a shelf and thought once I got our Colorado operation closed, I would return to "my baby, my Sherpa project."

A few weeks ago I met a young man by the name of T-Rex. His name is actually Thaddeus Rex. He's a younger man, a brand guy, smart, and has helped a few folks really streamline and target their brand.

We met for a cocktail, I shared my story, and he had an assessment. I gave him a few dead presidents and took a brand assessment on "The Insurance Sherpa."

I met with T-Rex this past Monday at my home. We reviewed the results of my vision, my work thus far, and my long-term plans and goals for "my brand."

T-Rex shared with me the following:

My brand was ill-conceived, not well thought out, was not laser focused, and I had really failed at my mission to create the platform I intended.

So this past Monday I killed my Sherpa dream. I don't know exactly my "sunk costs", but I know it was over $5,000.00 of my money I invested in the dream. After working with Thaddeus, it became clear that my dream was simply a distraction from my economic engine. My economic engine is The Thompson Group.

So, I failed. I'll keep my site up. I'll let it gather dust and if you are an independent agent, you might get a little "free value" from visiting my site.

I learned a few lessons, what not to do, what I could have done, and what I need to do if I ever get to a point where I can return to my dream.

But for now, I'm happy with my journey of the Sherpa, but know it best to let it die.

Sometimes in life, we get invested in a thing, project, or even a person and keep fighting even when we know it's a lost cause.

If you are working on a noun, a person, place, or thing and it is not or they are not performing as they need to perform, it is better to pull the plug and review your "sunk costs."

I'm mentoring a young individual right now and I'm not so sure they are going to make it.

They continue to make poor choices, live in a world that is not conducive to success and they can't seem to keep simple promises they have made to help them get their life on track.

Just like the Sherpa, I fear that my investment has been wasted, but I'm not afraid to end our relationship even though I've made a pretty substantial investment of my time in trying to improve the life of someone in need.

We all have dreams, but sometimes dreams must die so you can focus your attention on those nouns that will embrace and adopt your teachings and lessons.

Assess everything you are doing. What's working and what do you need to stop doing to help make your life more impactful?

This is not my last $5,000.00 plus mistake, but I seem to learn more from my mistakes than I ever learn from my successes.

If I fail in my mentorship of my young professional, I'll learn lessons as to what not to do with my future mentor students.

Focus, assess, and constantly ask yourself "is this the best use of my time?"

Be honest, cut bait, and move on. I did, I will, and for me, that has made all the difference.

"No matter where you go or what you do to distract yourself, reality catches up with you eventually."
— **Kody Keplinger**

I'll think about it – Doers and "Think About" Folk

"Twenty years from now you will be more disappointed by the things that you didn't do than by the ones you did do. So, throw off the bowlines. Sail away from the safe harbor. Catch the trade winds in your sails. Explore. Dream. Discover."
— **H. Jackson Brown Jr.**

There are two types of people: people that think about it and people that do it.

We all think, but few of us do. Doers succeed and "think about it" folk complain that nothing ever happens.

If you say you are going to do it, do it.

If you simply think about it and never do it, it might be why you are sitting in your current pool of misery.

It's Wednesday, July 19, 2017. Quit just thinking and start doing.

I did, I do, and for me, that has made all the difference.

Sleeping on my couch, there is a 25-year-old young man. He's a professional golfer. He's my nephew, and he works his ass off.

He thinks, and then he does. He in Colorado for a tournament that has a top prize of $100,000.00.

I think he might win that money. Nicky P. is a doer.

He gets up early, practices daily, manages his nutrition, his alcohol intake, and is positioned for success.

Nick, again, is 25. He's on a path to success not because he thinks about it, but he does it.

Stop bitching, moaning, and complaining and start doing things that will position you for success. Life is not that hard if you simply do.

"Twenty years from now you will be more disappointed by the things that you didn't do than by the ones you did do. So, throw off the bowlines. Sail away from the safe harbor. Catch the trade winds in your sails. Explore. Dream. Discover."
— **H. Jackson Brown Jr.**

Are you a DOER or a LEADER?

"The mediocre teacher tells. The good teacher explains. The superior teacher demonstrates. The great teacher inspires."
— **William Arthur Ward**

7:18 am in Colorado. I slept in! I would still be asleep but a client called our Parker City, Indiana office and needed help with a claim.

My streak of getting up at 5:00 am is over, I needed the sleep and my client needed help, so here I sit.

The claim has been turned in, the client is moving to stage two of our claims process; he was a little shocked someone answered the phone on a Saturday, but that is what we do.

I had a coaching call yesterday. My every other week call with my YODA, my wise one, my listener, my personal life Sherpa.

I'm moving from one position in life to another. For the past few years, I have been the lead producer in my agency. But as we grow, I know I need to begin transitioning my sales efforts to more sales support, focus on my existing client base, and start helping our newer team members hit their goals.

My coach asked, "Is it more important that you hit your sales goal or your team hits their sales goal?"

Ask me this a few years ago and I would have quickly said, "me, my, me, me, me, me, me, me, me, me," but yesterday I slowly said "them."

I'm moving from me to them. As a young lad, I also thought I would be a doer. I love doing. I love sales, but at this point in my career, I have a book of clients that understand my skill set, my team, our process and our services.

Instead of bringing on more "new clients" to my book of business, it's time to help every other team member reach his or her maximum personal and professional potential.

I brought in a new client this week and will continue doing so the next few years, but my focus is no longer new client development, it's the personal and professional development of my team.

If you work with us, you get me. Like it or not, I'm going to work with you to see if I can push you to be the best person you can be.

I've been working with one of our new team members for the last few months. They had no sales experience, no insurance experience, and at 28 years old had floated through life mastering many unique talents, but few that translated to the business world.

Over the past few months, I've watched this person that had very little organizational skills begin to get organized.

I've watched this person make sales call after sales call improving her approach every time she picked up the phone.

I've watched this person walk into businesses and talk to strangers with amazing results.

I'm juiced about our team member's personal development and think we found a rock star.

In the last 3 months, we have had 3 new team members join our family. All younger, motivated, and excited people wanting to personally and professionally grow.

I've lived much of my life as a selfish, self-centered, me-first individual. It's served me well, offended and turned off many I'm sure, but today I'm able to put my wants, needs, and desires second behind those needs of my team.

I'm 47 years old, I'll die at 114 so that is 67 years that I will have to work with my folks, my growing team, creating a company like no other.

I'm finally moving from a doer to a leader. I am in a different phase of life with 3 kids in college. No longer spending my evenings and weekends at the cross country meet, basketball game, or volleyball match.

My time is now my time and I can do with it what I want. So, today and tomorrow I'm going to hike. I'm going to challenge myself physically and mentally.

I'll push myself so when I work with my team, I can help push them past their comfort zone into places that will force personal and professional growth.

If you own a company, join me in moving past that of a doer and into that leadership position.

One of the cornerstone books that helped launch me to where I sit today (on a cheeseburger bean bag chair in a high rise in Denver, Colorado) was the book the E-Myth Revisited by Michael Gerber.

That book put me on a trajectory of personal and professional development so that when I needed to transition from doer to leader, I was ready.

I'm ready. I'm excited for this next new phase of my life. Connecting with new people that want to change their life. The vehicle we use to help propel one from where they are to where they want to be is our company called The Thompson Group.

It's not just a company, it's a life incubator for anyone that wants to improve their life.

We are very selective when bringing on new team members, but we will be doing so more frequently now with our western expansion.

Do as much as you can, but at some point, you need to begin doing less and leading more. I've arrived and I suspect many of my readers have as well.

Recognize when this change is needed. Begin slowly making the move from the main doer to the leader and watch as your company begins building on not just financial success, but the more important area of success: the personal development of every person that joins your organization.

"The mediocre teacher tells. The good teacher explains. The superior teacher demonstrates. The great teacher inspires."
— **William Arthur Ward**

Living a Double Life – Coming Out of the Closet

"I hope you have not been leading a double life, pretending to be wicked and being good all the time. That would be hypocrisy."
— **Oscar Wilde**

I live a double life. I'm not embarrassed about it. Most of my friends know my lifestyle. I think most people fear the double life, but for my partner and me, we have embraced this unique existence.

I lived in Indiana for 42 years. I was raised in a small town of 1,323 human beings, later moved to Indianapolis, but have spent most of my life in the Midwest.

At 42, I took a trip to Boulder, Colorado with my children and that trip changed my life. I spent the next 3 years returning to Boulder and Denver and began working during my visits. Something pulled me to Colorado, I hear others feel the same.

My partner and I decided to open up an office and try our luck at a scratch business.

Our goal was to find a similar type business to ours in Indiana, acquire it, and then grow from that acquisition.

Today, we are the owners of The Thompson Group with offices in Parker City, Indiana,

Indianapolis, Indiana, and now Denver, Colorado.

The first and third week of every month, my partner and I join our friends at Southwest Airlines and fly to our downtown condo in Denver.

We have an office in Stapleton; we work all over the city of Denver and surrounding communities.

The upsides of our double life include experiencing two very unique cultures. It has forced our Indiana team to step up and take over more responsibility as Jenny and I push west.

Our minds have been expanded whilst in Denver and combining this mind expansion with our Midwestern work ethic has proven a good formula for personal and professional growth.

The downside, of course, is our weekly 3-hour commute from doorstep to doorstep, but we tend to use our travel time effectively reviewing client information, company financials, and planning our next week or month.

You can't be sick or out of shape when straddling two states so we have been hyper focused on nutrition and exercise.

Our mindset is adjusted each time we visit our Denver community. We are coming from a situation of a strong brand and reputation to a position as an unknown commodity.

The established brand owner works and thinks different than a start-up. There are lessons to be learned from both positions and the lessons provide value to our entire company.

Our time in Denver has exposed us to a new way of working. The business community in Denver is a very small collection of key individuals.

They work differently in Denver than in the Midwest. There seems to be more open collaboration and sharing ideas between firms.

Groups like Colorado Thought Leaders Forum (CTLF) highlight the Denver community's commitment to providing education and exposing the limitless potential of a well-organized collaborative environment.

If our story inspires you to open an office or expand your company to a new state or territory, here's a few things you need to know.

It will take longer than you think to begin getting traction in your new market. Be patient.

Giving of yourself, knowledge, and sharing your experience from your "other life" can help both of your communities.

Stay organized. I use a virtual assistant to help me track the new people we have met since moving to Denver. Also, stay in touch with the people that helped build your company and that are allowing you to expand your reach.

Enjoy the journey. Although a unique existence, the living of a double life is filled with unique experiences, learning opportunities, and lessons that should be shared.

I hope these words have expanded your mind. Remember anything is possible. If you have a dream, follow it. It won't be easy, but no dream is easy. Develop a plan, execute that plan, and please, enjoy the journey.

"I hope you have not been leading a double life, pretending to be wicked and being good all the time. That would be hypocrisy."
— **Oscar Wilde**

Doubt Everything... Stop Living in the Dark

"Doubt everything. Find your own light."
— **Gautama Buddha**

5:23 am. Coconut oil infused coffee in hand. It's dark outside, soon the light will begin to show itself.

The light is hiding. It's not lights turn to show up. But soon, very soon, it will begin lighting the mountains to the west.

Right now you might be living in a dark time. A time when nothing seems to be going your way. You might think the world is against you, but you are simply living in the dark.

Life ebbs and flows through darkness and light. If things are not going your way, just wait, the light will soon appear and things will improve.

No matter your current state of affairs, I'd like to ask you to enjoy the experience. Enjoy your journey. There is no prize waiting for you at the end of your life, the prize is the journey you travel every day.

Life's prize is the good and the bad things that happen to every human being.

The beautiful thing about your life is that you are in complete control. You can actually decide to turn on a light when things are dark.

To turn on the light, you need to find out what is causing the darkness.

I got a call from a friend yesterday. He's in a relationship with a young lady. The young lady is drinking a little too much.

She can't just have one or two glasses of wine, his friend needs the entire bottle. When they go out, he knows he might be carrying her home, passed out from over consumption.

He was calling asking for some advice as to how to help her. She's aware this is a problem but has not yet committed to fixing the issue.

My advice was to not tell her to quit drinking. Humans don't respond well to orders or strong recommendations.

He needs to formulate a few questions and get her thinking about why she feels the need to drink herself to oblivion.

Honestly, her drinking is not the problem. Her drinking is masking the real problem.

If you drink too much, you probably don't do it because you like waking up feeling like crap. You know it's not healthy, but for some reason, you refuse to deal with the problem that is pushing you to daily numb your mind with fermented liquids.

I recommended to my friend to join her on a sober test. Take a few days sans booze and see how life improves. What is that nagging little issue that must be dealt with when sober?

My friend's girlfriend is living in the dark. The light is available, but she prefers to live in the dark.

Many times we choose to live in the dark knowing the source of light, the little sliver of light that can make our world so much better.

This morning, I ask that you stop living in the dark. No matter your life path, there is a path that is well lit. There is a path that can be taken that will shine bright and allow you to see all the amazing things that you are failing to see due to your choice to live in the darkness.

Good luck, it's the start of another amazing week. A light-filled journey of opportunities, new experiences, and new people that could change your life.

Enjoy the darkness for it's just as important as the light, but find your switch.

I'm off to change the world. Join me, won't you?

"Doubt everything. Find your own light."
— **Gautama Buddha**

Drag Show, Social Media, and an Appreciation for Life

"I believe that everything happens for a reason. People change so that you can learn to let go, things go wrong so that you appreciate them when they're right, you believe lies so you eventually learn to trust no one but yourself, and sometimes good things fall apart so better things can fall together."
— **Marilyn Monroe**

I attended my first drag show last night. It was at a club in Fort Lauderdale, Florida. It was called Lips and as a 48-year-old heterosexual male, I had a blast.

The place was packed, the food was good, the drinks were cold and the performances were well done. The host was fantastic and we had an amazing time.

We returned home to sit outside, sip a little wine and chat. It was a small group, our daughter, her boyfriend, my Queen, and our cousin.

We started talking about how the world has changed since we were young. How the kids today have such an advantage, so much more of an understanding of our world.

Let's be honest, there are no more questions. Any question you have can be answered by asking Siri, Google, or Alexa. If you need knowledge, it's free on demand.

I got my first cell phone when I was 22. For those of you youngsters that are reading this, I was not poor, people just didn't have cell phones.

No one had a cell phone. Imagine the world sans cell phones.

So, let's go back, back, back to a time where there were no cell phones, no voice mail, no pagers, just a land-line phone at your home or business.

You would see people in public but there were no social media updates. You caught up on the phone or if you happened to connect with a friend or family member. We lived very private lives before cell phones.

As a kid, I had a good friend. I would call his house to see if he was home. If he didn't pick up or if the people on his party line picked up, I had to wait until he got home to chat with him.

If the term party line is confusing, Google it. It was a thing back in the day.

I didn't know where he was, I couldn't check social media to see when he might be home. I had to simply wait until Brad got home and answered my call so we could go on an adventure.

While home, I had 3 channels on our television, I didn't watch much TV, and there was not much to watch. I would go out, climb a tree, maybe ride my bike over to another friend's house.

The times were much different.

Today, we are connected. I talked to all 3 of my kids yesterday. My son and daughter were in Indiana. I face-timed them, we had a nice chat; facetime is an amazing tool, I'm never far from my family or loved ones.

I sent a few snap chats to my family and friends allowing them to see what I was seeing. A lot of videos on the beach, a few stories from our pool time, and of course, stories from the drag show.

I live an open book life, fully transparent, letting the world know what I'm doing. I live an interesting life and I like to share my life with my family and friends.

20 years ago, it would have been impossible to live the life I lead today. I could not have traveled back and forth 1,108 miles between homes.

It would be hard to jump on a plane and go visit a kid 6 states away. Travel by plane is now as simple as getting in your car.

I could not have been in touch with my office and my staff 6 states away. I would never see my family or friends, I would guess that air travel 20 years ago would have been much different without the likes of Southwest.

I think we forget how fast times have changed and how many tools we now have at our disposal to make our lives richer and more complete.

You can work from anywhere in the world. You can keep connected with hundreds or thousands of people.

With the internet, you can keep track of your company, friends, family, and keep connected to your clients.

People like to complain about our current state of affairs. They point to all the evil and perceived corruption. We want to focus on things like those damn Russians, that Antichrist Trump, or our health insurance options.

But if we stop and think about how far we have come with technology and all the benefits we have versus what we had in the 80's or 90's, we live in an amazing time.

Today, pick up your phone and face-time your parents or kids. Post an update on social media to let the world know what you are up to.

Write a blog and post it on LinkedIn or share a story on snap chat. Tweet, or share a photo of your cat, dog, or new sex toy on Instagram.

Take a day and enjoy the world around you. Do something weird like attend a drag show, connect with an old friend, but don't bitch and moan.

We are living in an amazing time, enjoy the fucking journey.

"I believe that everything happens for a reason. People change so that you can learn to let go, things go wrong so that you appreciate them when they're right, you believe lies so you eventually learn to trust no one but yourself, and sometimes good things fall apart so better things can fall together."
— **Marilyn Monroe**

Drama – It's Your Choice

"People don't want their lives fixed. Nobody wants their problems solved. Their dramas. their distractions. Their stories resolved. Their messes cleaned up. Because what would they have left? Just the big scary unknown."
— **Chuck Palahniuk**

There is no place in this world for drama. Well, Broadway, the movies, Netflix, but outside of entertainment, drama must be nipped in the bud.

There are people, you know these people, that live drama filled lives. Everything is a big deal. The world is scheming against them. If the world leaves them alone, they are pushing buttons trying to get the drama machine running again at full speed.

I have found a solution for the drama kings and queens in my life. The solution is to no longer allow them in my life.

Life is meant to be a joyful journey. It can be a joyful journey if you choose it to be joyful.

Some folks aren't happy unless they are miserable. You know this person. You know these people. As you read these words, these faces and names are filling your head.

These people are the first to reach out when tragedy strikes somehow feeding off other's misfortune. They need details. Drama folks love details.

Here's an idea. Let's take all the drama filled people and give them a state. They can bitch, complain, moan, and cause chaos in the lives of other drama loving people.

They can stay out of the lives of those of us that choose light and happiness over darkness and sadness.

Drama based folks like to stir up trouble. They are usually the first ones to know "the news" and they love to share said news.

Drama folks like to say "did you hear about...?" They seem to know bits and bytes about almost everyone and like to share those little tidbits to whoever will listen.

Drama folks like to talk out of school. Sharing information that need not be shared, but they simply can't help themselves. That information is their power. It's all they have.

It's Friday, share this message with your family, your loved ones, and your inner circle. Send a message to those that lean toward drama and let them know it is no longer going to be tolerated.

We are what we tolerate and thus, I no longer tolerate drama. I'm asking you consider making this choice as well.

"People don't want their lives fixed. Nobody wants their problems solved. Their dramas. their distractions. Their stories resolved. Their messes cleaned up. Because what would they have left? Just the big scary unknown."
— **Chuck Palahniuk**

60674568R00133

Made in the USA
Columbia, SC
16 June 2019